9x13

A Plan for Your Pan

120 one-size-fits-all recipes

Printed in the United States of America
by G&R Publishing Co.

Distributed By:

507 Industrial Street
Waverly, IA 50677

ISBN-13: 978-1-56383-385-4
ISBN-10: 1-56383-385-9
Item #7062

Table of Contents

9 x 13

There are nearly as many types of 9 x 13" pans as there are ways to use them. Let these quick tips help you choose the best pan for each recipe.

- Glass pans and pans with dark-colored finishes are generally the best for creating a deep brown baked surface. These finishes absorb heat in the oven.

- Light and bright-surface pans work well for non-baked items or baked items that don't require intense browning such as egg-based casseroles or cheese-covered dishes.

- Plastic pans – while traditionally created for non-baked items – are now available for oven use.

- Nonstick pans should be used for items that will be removed from the pan before cutting to prevent scratching of the nonstick surface.

- Silicone pans are lightweight and flexible, making them easy to handle, transport and store. When filled, however, they should be placed on another pan to move them to and from the oven and may need a longer baking time.

No matter what types of 9 x 13" pans you have, the following pages will assure you have a way to use them!

What's the plan for YOUR pan?

Breakfasts

Sausage & Egg Bake

makes 12 servings

Ingredients

1 lb. Italian sausage links, casings removed

1 sweet green bell pepper, chopped

1 onion, chopped

1 (16 oz.) container cottage cheese

2 C. shredded Cheddar cheese

1½ C. egg substitute

1 C. milk

1 C. baking mix

1 (4 oz.) can diced green chiles, drained

Preparation

Preheat oven to 350°. Spray a 9 x 13″ baking pan with nonstick cooking spray; set aside. In a large nonstick skillet over medium heat, cook sausage, bell pepper and onion until meat is no longer pink; drain. Stir in cottage cheese, Cheddar cheese, egg substitute, milk, baking mix and chile peppers. Pour egg mixture into prepared pan. Bake for 35 to 40 minutes or until a knife inserted near the center comes out clean. Let stand for 10 minutes before cutting and serving.

Egg Brunch Casserole

makes 12 servings

Ingredients

4 C. frozen shredded hash browns, thawed
1 tsp. salt
¼ tsp. garlic salt
½ tsp. pepper
1 lb. sliced bacon
1 T. butter

1 onion, chopped
2 C. sliced fresh mushrooms
4 eggs
1½ C. milk
1 tsp. dried parsley flakes
1 C. shredded Cheddar cheese

Preparation

Spray a 9 x 13″ baking pan with nonstick cooking spray. Pour hash browns evenly into prepared pan. Sprinkle with salt, garlic salt and pepper. In a medium nonstick skillet over medium heat, fry bacon until crisp; drain and crumble. Sprinkle bacon evenly over hash browns. Meanwhile, in another medium skillet over medium heat, melt butter. Add onion and mushrooms; cook until tender. Pour evenly over bacon. In a large bowl, beat eggs with milk and parsley; pour over mixture in pan. Top with cheese. Refrigerate overnight.

Preheat oven to 400°. Bake for 1 hour or until set. Let stand for 10 minutes before cutting into squares.

Down-Home Casserole

makes 12 servings

Ingredients

6 C. frozen shredded hash browns, thawed

1½ C. shredded Pepper Jack cheese

2 C. Canadian-style bacon

½ C. sliced green onion

8 eggs, lightly beaten

2 (12 oz.) cans evaporated milk

¼ tsp. salt

¼ tsp. pepper

Preparation

Preheat oven to 350°. Spray a 9 x 13″ baking pan with nonstick cooking spray. Pour hash browns evenly into prepared pan. Sprinkle with cheese, Canadian-style bacon and onion. In a large bowl, whisk together eggs, milk, salt and pepper; pour over cheese mixture in pan. Bake for 45 to 55 minutes or until set. Let stand for 5 minutes before cutting and serving.

Biscuit & Egg Bake

makes 12 servings

Ingredients

1 (16.3 oz.) tube large refrigerated buttermilk biscuits, such as Grands

12 eggs

1 C. milk

1 C. chopped fresh tomato

½ C. chopped green onion

1 (4 oz.) can diced green chiles, drained

1 tsp. salt

½ tsp. pepper

½ tsp. garlic powder

1 (2.1 oz.) pkg. fully cooked bacon, diced

2 C. shredded Cheddar cheese

Preparation

Preheat oven to 350°. Spray a 9 x 13″ baking pan with nonstick cooking spray. Separate biscuits and cut each into fourths; arrange in prepared pan. In a medium bowl, whisk together eggs, milk, tomato, onion, chile peppers, salt, pepper and garlic powder. Pour over biscuits in pan. Sprinkle with bacon and cheese. Bake for 40 to 45 minutes or until golden brown. Let stand for 10 minutes before cutting and serving.

Caramel Cinnamon Rolls

makes 15 servings

Ingredients

1 C. plus 2 T. milk, divided
1½ tsp. active dry yeast
2 T. sugar
1 egg
6 T. plus ⅓ C. butter, divided
½ tsp. salt

3⅓ C. bread flour
1 C. brown sugar, divided
1½ C. chopped walnuts, divided
2 tsp. ground cinnamon
½ C. raisins

Preparation

In a small saucepan over low heat, heat 1 cup milk until it reaches 105° to 115°. In a large mixing bowl, stir together warm milk, yeast and sugar until dissolved; let stand for 10 minutes. Add egg, 2 tablespoons butter, salt and flour. With a dough hook, mix on low speed for 4 to 5 minutes. Grease a 9 x 13″ baking pan and set aside. In a medium saucepan over medium-low heat, melt ⅓ cup butter. Stir in ½ cup brown sugar, 2 tablespoons milk and 1 cup walnuts. Stir constantly until well blended. Spread mixture evenly in prepared pan. Place dough on a lightly floured surface and roll out to a 10 x 15″ rectangle. In a small microwave-safe bowl, melt remaining ¼ cup butter; brush on dough. Sprinkle with remaining ½ cup brown sugar, remaining ½ cup walnuts, cinnamon and raisins. Roll up jelly roll style starting with a long side; press edges to seal. With a knife, cut the roll into 15 (1″) pieces. Place dough pieces cut side down on top of caramel mixture. Cover with a damp cloth and let rise in a warm place until double in size, 1½ to 2 hours.

Preheat oven to 350°. Bake for 15 to 20 minutes or until golden brown. Remove from oven and immediately turn upside down on a large pan or serving plate. Serve warm or cold.

Quick Cinnamon Rolls

makes 15 servings

Ingredients

1 (1 lb.) loaf frozen bread
   dough, thawed
3 T. butter, divided
⅔ C. brown sugar
½ C. chopped pecans
1 tsp. ground cinnamon

⅔ C. whipping cream
1 C. powdered sugar, sifted
Pinch of salt
½ tsp. vanilla extract
1 to 2 T. milk

Preparation

Grease a 9 x 13" baking pan and set aside. On a lightly floured surface, roll thawed dough out to a 6 x 15˝ rectangle. Melt 2 tablespoons butter and brush onto dough. In a small bowl, stir together brown sugar, pecans and cinnamon; sprinkle evenly over dough. Roll up jelly roll style starting with a long side; press edges to seal. With a knife or unflavored dental floss, cut the roll into 15 (1˝) pieces. Place dough pieces cut side down in prepared pan. Cover with a damp cloth and let rise in a warm place until double in size, about 1 hour.

Preheat oven to 350°. Pour whipping cream evenly over rolls. Bake for 25 to 30 minutes or until golden brown. Remove from oven and immediately turn upside down on a large pan or serving plate. In a small microwave-safe bowl, melt remaining 1 tablespoon butter. Add powdered sugar, salt and vanilla, stirring in milk a little at a time to drizzling consistency. Drizzle icing over warm rolls. Serve rolls warm or cold.

Breakfast Pizza

makes 8 to 10 servings

Ingredients

1 (6.5 oz.) box pizza crust mix
1 lb. ground sausage
1 C. chopped fresh tomato
½ lb. fresh mushrooms, sliced
1½ C. shredded mozzarella
    cheese, divided

1½ C. shredded sharp
    Cheddar cheese, divided
4 eggs
Salt and pepper to taste
Salsa, optional

Preparation

Preheat oven to 350°. Spray a 9 x 13″ baking pan with nonstick cooking spray; set aside. Prepare crust mix according to package directions. Spread dough in prepared pan, covering the bottom and 2″ up the sides; set aside. In a medium skillet over medium heat, cook sausage until no longer pink; drain well. Spread over dough in pan. Top with tomato, mushrooms, 1 cup mozzarella cheese and 1 cup Cheddar cheese. Bake for 8 to 10 minutes or until crust edges are golden brown. Remove from oven. In a small bowl, whisk together eggs, salt and pepper; pour over cheese in pan. Return pan to oven and bake for an additional 7 to 9 minutes or until eggs are set. Immediately sprinkle with remaining ½ cup mozzarella and Cheddar cheeses. Cut in squares and serve hot with salsa, if desired.

Cheesy Chile Puff

Ingredients

¾ C. flour
1½ tsp. baking powder
9 eggs
1 lb. shredded Monterey
  Jack cheese
2 C. cottage cheese

2 (4 oz.) cans diced
  green chiles, drained
1½ tsp. sugar
¼ tsp. salt
⅛ tsp. hot pepper sauce
1 C. salsa

Preparation

Preheat oven to 350°. Spray a 9 x 13″ baking pan with nonstick cooking spray; set aside. In a small bowl, stir together flour and baking powder. In a large bowl, whisk eggs; stir in Monterey Jack cheese, cottage cheese, chile peppers, sugar, salt and hot pepper sauce. Add flour mixture, stirring until just combined. Pour into prepared pan. Bake for 45 minutes or until egg mixture is set. Let stand for 5 minutes before cutting and serving. Serve with salsa.

Cheesy Veggie Frittata

makes 8 to 10 servings

Ingredients

3 T. vegetable oil

1½ C. chopped zucchini

1½ C. chopped fresh
mushrooms

¾ C. chopped onion

¾ C. chopped sweet green
bell pepper

1 clove garlic, minced

9 eggs

¼ C. half-and-half

2 (8 oz.) pkgs. cream cheese,
softened, cubed

2 C. shredded Cheddar cheese

4 slices whole wheat bread,
cubed

1 tsp. salt

¼ tsp. pepper

Preparation

Preheat oven to 350°. Spray a 9 x 13″ baking pan with nonstick
cooking spray; set aside. Heat vegetable oil in a large skillet
over medium-high heat. Add zucchini, mushrooms, onion, bell
pepper and garlic; sauté until tender and remove from heat. In a
large bowl, whisk together eggs and half-and-half. Stir in cream
cheese cubes, Cheddar cheese, bread cubes, salt, pepper and
vegetable mixture; mix well. Pour into prepared pan. Bake for
1 hour or until eggs are set. Cut into squares to serve.

Spinach & Cheese Quiche

makes 8 to 10 servings

Ingredients

1 (11 oz.) box pie crust mix

1 (10 oz.) pkg. frozen chopped spinach, thawed, well drained

1 (2.8 oz.) can French fried onions

1 C. shredded Swiss cheese

1 (8 oz.) container sour cream

5 eggs

1 C. milk

1 T. prepared spicy brown mustard

½ tsp. salt

⅛ tsp. pepper

Preparation

Preheat oven to 400°. Line a 9 x 13″ baking pan with aluminum foil and spray foil with nonstick cooking spray; set aside. In a large bowl, combine crust mix and ⅓ cup water until moistened and crumbly. Press mixture firmly in prepared pan using the bottom of a measuring cup dipped in flour. Prick crust several times with a fork. Bake for 20 minutes or until golden. Remove from oven and reduce oven temperature to 350°. Layer spinach, French fried onions and cheese over crust. In a medium bowl, combine sour cream, eggs, milk, mustard, salt and pepper; mix until well blended. Pour over cheese in pan. Bake for 30 minutes or until a knife inserted near the center comes out clean. Let stand for 10 minutes before cutting and serving.

Apple Strata

makes 8 to 10 servings

Ingredients

½ lb. sausage links, casings removed
4 C. cubed French bread
2 C. diced peeled apples*
¼ C. sliced green onion
⅓ C. sliced pitted ripe olives
1½ C. shredded sharp Cheddar cheese

2 C. milk
8 eggs
2 tsp. prepared spicy brown mustard
½ tsp. salt
¼ tsp. pepper
Paprika, optional

Preparation

Spray a 9 x 13″ baking pan with nonstick cooking spray; set aside. In a small skillet over medium-high heat, brown sausage until no longer pink; drain well. Layer half the bread cubes in prepared pan. Crumble sausage over bread and top with apples, onion, olives and cheese. Cover with remaining half the bread cubes. In a medium bowl, whisk together milk, eggs, mustard, salt and pepper; pour over bread. Cover with aluminum foil and refrigerate overnight.

Preheat oven to 350°. Bake covered for 45 minutes. Remove foil and bake for 15 minutes more or until center is set. Let stand for 15 minutes before cutting and serving. Sprinkle with paprika, if desired.

Gala, Jonathan or McIntosh work well.

Kielbasa Strata

makes 6 servings

Ingredients

6 eggs
1½ C. milk
2 T. prepared yellow mustard
½ tsp. dried sage
½ tsp. salt
¼ tsp. pepper
12 thick slices white bread

½ lb. kielbasa,
   cut into ½″ slices
1 (10 oz.) pkg. frozen
   chopped spinach,
   thawed, well drained
2 C. shredded Swiss cheese

Preparation

Preheat oven to 375°. Spray a 9 x 13″ baking pan with nonstick cooking spray; set aside. In a large bowl, whisk together eggs, milk, mustard, sage, salt and pepper. Add bread slices and press down gently. Remove six slices, letting excess drip back into bowl, and lay them in the bottom of prepared pan. Top with half each of the kielbasa, spinach and cheese. Place remaining six bread slices on top and repeat layers. Pour egg mixture over all. Bake covered for 15 minutes. Uncover and bake 15 minutes more. Cut and serve.

Ham & Swiss Strata

makes 8 to 10 servings

Ingredients

Butter for greasing pan
1 lb. Italian bread, crust removed
1 C. diced ham
2 C. shredded Swiss cheese
2 T. minced fresh chives

2 tomatoes, sliced ¼″ thick
8 eggs
4 C. milk
2 T. prepared Dijon mustard
2 tsp. coarse salt
¼ tsp. pepper

Preparation

Grease a 9 x 13″ baking pan with butter. Cut bread crosswise into ½″ slices. Arrange half of the bread in prepared pan. Sprinkle with half each of the ham, cheese and chives. Add another layer of bread and cover with remaining half of the ham, cheese and chives. Arrange tomato slices on top. In a large bowl, whisk together eggs, milk, mustard, salt and pepper until well combined; pour over mixture in pan. Refrigerate overnight.

Remove from refrigerator 25 minutes before baking. Meanwhile, preheat oven to 350°. Bake for 60 to 70 minutes or until a knife inserted near the center comes out clean. Let stand for 20 minutes before cutting and serving.

Morning Enchiladas

makes 10 to 12 servings

Ingredients

2 C. diced ham
½ C. chopped green onion
10 (8˝) flour tortillas
2 C. shredded Cheddar
  cheese, divided

1 T. flour
2 C. half-and-half
6 eggs, lightly beaten
¼ tsp. salt

Preparation

Spray a 9 x 13˝ baking pan with nonstick cooking spray; set aside. In a small bowl, stir together ham and onion. Sprinkle about ⅓ cup mixture down the center of each tortilla. Top each with 2 tablespoons cheese. Roll up and place seam side down in prepared pan. In a medium bowl, whisk together flour, half-and-half, eggs and salt until smooth. Pour over tortillas in pan. Refrigerate overnight.

Remove from refrigerator 30 minutes before baking. Meanwhile, preheat oven to 350°. Bake covered for 25 minutes; uncover and bake for 10 minutes more. Sprinkle with remaining ¾ cup cheese. Bake for 3 minutes more or until cheese melts. Let stand for 10 minutes before cutting and serving.

Blueberry-Pecan Baked French Toast

makes 6 servings

Ingredients

1 (1 lb.) loaf day-old egg
    bread, such as brioche
5 eggs
2½ C. milk
1 C. brown sugar, divided
1 tsp. vanilla extract

½ tsp. ground nutmeg
1 C. chopped pecans
¼ C. melted butter
2 C. fresh or frozen and
    thawed blueberries

Preparation

Spray a 9 x 13˝ baking pan with nonstick cooking spray.
Cut bread into large cubes and arrange in prepared pan.
In a medium bowl, whisk together eggs, milk, ¾ cup brown
sugar, vanilla and nutmeg; pour over bread in pan.
Refrigerate overnight.

Remove from refrigerator 30 minutes before baking. Preheat
oven to 375°. Sprinkle pecans over egg mixture. In a small bowl,
combine butter and remaining ¼ cup brown sugar; drizzle
over pecans. Bake for 25 to 30 minutes. Remove from oven and
sprinkle with blueberries. Increase oven temperature to 400°
and bake for 10 minutes more or until a knife inserted near the
center comes out clean. Let stand for 10 minutes before serving.

Overnight French Toast with Apples

makes 6 servings

Ingredients

1 C. brown sugar
½ C. butter
2 T. light corn syrup
2 tart apples, such as
  Granny Smith, peeled
  and sliced ¼" thick
3 eggs
1 C. milk

1 tsp. vanilla extract
9 (¾" thick) slices day-old
  French bread
1 C. applesauce
1 (10 oz.) jar apple jelly
½ tsp. ground cinnamon
⅛ tsp. ground cloves

Preparation

In a small saucepan over medium heat, combine brown sugar, butter and corn syrup. Cook and stir for 5 to 7 minutes or until thickened. Pour mixture into an ungreased 9 x 13" baking pan. Arrange apple slices over brown sugar mixture. In a medium bowl, combine eggs, milk and vanilla; mix well. Dip bread slices in egg mixture, letting soak for about 1 minute. Place bread slices over apples in pan, cutting and fitting bread to fit. Refrigerate overnight.

Remove from refrigerator 30 minutes before baking. Meanwhile, preheat oven to 350°. Bake for 35 to 40 minutes. In a medium saucepan over medium heat, combine applesauce, jelly, cinnamon and cloves. Cook and stir until thoroughly heated. To serve, place French toast on serving plates and cover with hot applesauce mixture.

Cherry Coffee Cake

makes 12 to 15 servings

Ingredients

1 (18.2 oz.) pkg. yellow
cake mix, divided
1 C. flour
1 (.25 oz.) pkg. active dry yeast
2 eggs, lightly beaten

1 (21 oz.) can cherry pie filling
⅓ C. butter, cubed
1 C. powdered sugar
1 T. light corn syrup

Preparation

Preheat oven to 350°. Spray a 9 x 13˝ baking pan with nonstick cooking spray; set aside. In a large bowl, combine 1½ cups dry cake mix, flour, yeast and ⅔ cup warm water, stirring until smooth. Stir in eggs until well blended. Spread mixture evenly in prepared pan. Spread pie filling evenly over mixture in pan. Pour remaining dry cake mix into a small bowl. Use a pastry blender to cut in butter until mixture resembles coarse crumbs. Sprinkle over pie filling. Bake for 35 to 40 minutes or until lightly browned. Cool on a wire rack. Meanwhile, in a small bowl, stir together powdered sugar, corn syrup and enough water to make a drizzling consistency. Drizzle over cake before cutting and serving.

Sunshine Lemon Coffee Cake

makes 12 to 15 servings

Ingredients

6 T. flour, divided

1 (18.2 oz.) pkg. lemon cake mix

¾ C. egg substitute

⅓ C. unsweetened applesauce

3 T. poppy seed

Flour for dusting

1 (8 oz.) pkg. cream cheese, softened

1 C. powdered sugar, divided

1 (15.75 oz.) can lemon pie filling

⅓ C. brown sugar

¼ C. chopped pecans

4½ T. melted butter

½ tsp. ground cinnamon

⅛ tsp. vanilla extract

4 tsp. lemon juice

Preparation

Preheat oven to 350°. Spray a 9 x 13" baking pan with nonstick cooking spray . Dust with 3 tablespoons flour, shake out and discard excess. Set pan aside. In a large mixing bowl, beat cake mix, 1⅓ cups water, egg substitute, applesauce and poppy seed on low speed for 30 seconds. Beat on medium speed for 2 minutes. Spread half the mixture in prepared pan. In a clean large mixing bowl, beat cream cheese and ½ cup powdered sugar on medium speed until smooth. Stir in pie filling. Drop by teaspoonfuls over batter in pan; spread evenly. Top with remaining half the batter. In a small bowl, stir together brown sugar, pecans, remaining 3 tablespoons flour, butter, cinnamon and vanilla. Sprinkle over batter. Bake for 40 to 45 minutes or until a toothpick inserted near the center comes out clean. Cool on a wire rack. In a small bowl, combine remaining ½ cup powdered sugar and lemon juice, stirring until smooth. Drizzle over cake before serving. Store in refrigerator.

Graham Cracker Streusel Coffee Cake

makes 12 to 15 servings

Ingredients

1½ C. graham cracker crumbs
¾ C. brown sugar
¾ C. chopped pecans
1½ tsp. ground cinnamon
⅔ C. melted butter
1 (18.2 oz.) pkg.
   yellow cake mix

Eggs, oil and water according
   to cake mix directions
½ C. powdered sugar
1 tsp. vanilla extract
½ to 1 T. milk

Preparation

Preheat oven to 350°. Spray a 9 x 13" baking pan with nonstick cooking spray; set aside. In a small bowl, stir together cracker crumbs, brown sugar, pecans and cinnamon. Stir in butter; set aside. Prepare cake mix using eggs, oil and water according to package directions. Pour half of the batter into prepared pan; sprinkle with half of the cracker mixture. Carefully spread the remaining half of the batter on top and sprinkle with remaining half of the cracker mixture. Bake for 40 to 45 minutes or until a toothpick inserted near the center comes out clean. Cool on a wire rack. In a small bowl, combine powdered sugar, vanilla and milk. Stir until smooth and drizzle over coffee cake before serving.

Salads

Mediterranean Veggie Salad

makes 10 servings

Ingredients

6 C. torn mixed greens
1 C. crumbled feta cheese, divided
½ C. coarsely chopped pitted ripe olives
½ cucumber, sliced ¼" thick
1 carrot, peeled and shredded
½ C. finely chopped fresh parsley
½ C. mayonnaise
½ C. plain yogurt
1 tsp. finely grated orange peel
½ tsp. pepper
½ tsp. salt
1 orange, peeled, sliced
½ C. chopped pecans

Preparation

Arrange salad greens in a 9 x 13" pan. Add ½ cup cheese, olives, cucumber, shredded carrot and parsley. In a small bowl, whisk together mayonnaise, yogurt, orange peel, pepper and salt. Spread dressing over salad, covering completely. Sprinkle with remaining ½ cup cheese. Cover and refrigerate overnight. Garnish with orange slices and pecans before serving.

Loaded Layer Salad

makes 12 servings

Ingredients

2 C. mayonnaise

1 (1 oz.) pkg. buttermilk dressing mix

1 (8 oz.) container sour cream

1 lb. sliced bacon

½ lb. fresh spinach, torn into bite-size pieces

1 head lettuce, torn into bite-size pieces

½ C. chopped celery

6 hard-cooked eggs, chopped

1½ C. frozen peas, thawed

10 green onions, chopped

1 (8 oz.) can water chestnuts, drained

1½ C. shredded American cheese

Preparation

In a medium bowl, stir together mayonnaise, dressing mix and sour cream. Refrigerate overnight.

In a large skillet over medium heat, fry bacon until crisp; drain and crumble. In a 9 x 13″ pan, layer evenly spinach, lettuce, celery, eggs, peas, onions, bacon and water chestnuts. Pour chilled dressing mixture over salad in pan and sprinkle with cheese before serving.

Deep-Dish Layered Salad

makes 10 servings

Ingredients

1½ heads lettuce, shredded
1 C. chopped celery
1 C. chopped sweet
   red bell pepper
½ C. chopped red onion
2 C. sliced fresh mushrooms
2 C. frozen peas, thawed
4 hard-cooked eggs, chopped

2 C. mayonnaise
2 T. brown sugar
½ tsp. garlic powder
½ tsp. curry powder
2 T. bacon bits
2 T. grated Parmesan cheese

Preparation

Place half of the lettuce in a 9 x 13″ pan. Sprinkle with celery, bell pepper, onion, mushrooms, peas and eggs. Top with remaining half the lettuce. Refrigerate for several hours. In a small bowl, whisk together mayonnaise, brown sugar, garlic powder and curry powder. Spread evenly over lettuce in pan. Sprinkle with bacon bits and Parmesan cheese before serving.

Pea Salad

makes 10 servings

Ingredients

8 strips bacon
2 heads Romaine lettuce,
   torn into bite-size pieces
1 (16 oz.) pkg. frozen peas
8 hard-cooked eggs, sliced

2 C. mayonnaise
2 T. milk
3 T. sugar
3 C. shredded
   Cheddar cheese

Preparation

In a large skillet over medium heat, fry bacon until crisp; drain and crumble. Place lettuce evenly in a 9 x 13″ pan. Sprinkle lettuce with bacon, peas and eggs. In a small bowl, mix together mayonnaise, milk and sugar until smooth. Pour evenly over salad and top with cheese. Chill for 2 hours before serving.

Summer Salad

makes 10 servings

Ingredients

4 to 5 strips bacon
3 C. shredded red cabbage
3 C. sliced cauliflower
1½ cucumbers, sliced

1½ C. halved cherry tomatoes
½ lb. spinach, torn
   into bite-size pieces
1½ C. bottled onion dressing

Preparation

In a large skillet over medium heat, fry bacon until crisp; drain and crumble. In a 9 x 13″ pan, layer cabbage, cauliflower, cucumbers, tomatoes and spinach. Sprinkle with bacon. Pour dressing over all and refrigerate for several hours before serving.

Stacked Noodle Salad

makes 12 servings

Ingredients

1 (8 oz.) container sour cream

½ C. bottled peanut sauce

⅛ tsp. cayenne pepper, optional

½ (6 to 7 oz.) pkg. rice noodles, broken

1 C. fresh snap peas, trimmed

4 C. shredded Napa cabbage

¼ daikon or other mild white radish

2 C. broccoli slaw mix

½ C. chopped fresh cilantro

¼ C. coarsely chopped peanuts

Preparation

In a medium bowl, combine sour cream, peanut sauce and cayenne pepper, if desired; set aside. Prepare rice noodles according to package directions; drain. Rinse with cold water and drain again. Cook snap peas covered in a small amount of boiling salted water for 2 minutes until crisp-tender; drain. Rinse with cold water and drain again. In a 9 x 13" pan, layer cabbage, noodles, snap peas, daikon, broccoli slaw and cilantro. Carefully spread sour cream mixture over cilantro. Sprinkle with peanuts. Refrigerate until serving time, up to 8 hours.

Quickie Southwestern Layered Salad

makes 10 to 12 servings

Ingredients

6 C. Romaine lettuce, torn into bite-size pieces

1 (15 oz.) can black beans, drained, rinsed

1 (11 oz.) can whole-kernel corn, drained

½ C. thick salsa

¼ C. Monterey Jack cheese

¼ C. colby cheese

¼ C. Cheddar cheese

½ C. bottled ranch dressing

1 C. broken tortilla chips

Preparation

Place lettuce in a 9 x 13″ pan. Cover with layers of beans, corn and salsa. Add Monterey Jack, colby and Cheddar cheeses. Drizzle with dressing and sprinkle with chips. Serve immediately.

Potluck Layer Salad

makes 10 to 12 servings

Ingredients

- 4 C. torn mixed greens
- 1 (15 oz.) can garbanzo beans, rinsed, drained
- 1 C. halved cherry tomatoes
- 1 C. thinly sliced fresh fennel or celery
- 1 C. chopped sweet yellow bell pepper
- 1 C. diced ham
- ¼ C. thinly sliced green onion
- 1 C. mayonnaise
- 2 T. milk
- 1 tsp. fennel seed, crushed
- ⅛ tsp. white pepper
- ¾ C. shredded smoked Cheddar cheese

Preparation

In a 9 x 13" pan, layer mixed greens, garbanzo beans, tomatoes, fennel, bell pepper, ham and onion. In a small bowl, stir together mayonnaise, milk, fennel seed and pepper. Carefully spread mayonnaise mixture over salad in pan. Refrigerate overnight; sprinkle with cheese before serving.

Seafood Salad

makes 10 to 12 servings

Ingredients

4 C. shredded lettuce
2 C. fresh snow peas, cut
   into bite-size pieces
1 C. chopped cucumber
1½ C. chopped sweet
   red bell pepper
½ lb. cooked
   crabmeat or shrimp

1 C. mayonnaise
1 T. sugar
1 tsp. dillweed
1 (2.25 oz.) can sliced
   pitted ripe olives

Preparation

In a 9 x 13″ pan, layer lettuce, snow peas, cucumber, bell pepper and crabmeat. Refrigerate for several hours. In a small bowl, combine mayonnaise, sugar and dillweed; stir to mix well. Spread mixture evenly over salad. Refrigerate for several hours. At serving time, sprinkle with olives.

Hot Seafood Salad

makes 10 to 12 servings

Ingredients

2 C. sliced celery
½ C. chopped onion
1 sweet green bell pepper, chopped
1 (8 oz.) can sliced water chestnuts, drained
1 (6 oz.) can crabmeat, drained, flaked
1 (4 oz.) can shrimp, drained, chopped

1 (4 oz.) can mushrooms, drained
1 C. mayonnaise
4 hard-cooked eggs, sliced
½ tsp. salt
½ tsp. paprika
½ C. bread crumbs
¼ C. melted butter

Preparation

Preheat oven to 350°. Spray a 9 x 13″ baking pan with nonstick cooking spray; set aside. In a large bowl, combine celery, onion, bell pepper, water chestnuts, crabmeat, shrimp, mushrooms, mayonnaise, hard-cooked eggs, salt and paprika. Transfer mixture to prepared pan. Sprinkle with bread crumbs and drizzle with melted butter. Bake for 30 minutes or until heated through. Serve hot.

Cranberry Salad

makes 18 servings

Ingredients

2 (3 oz.) pkgs.
    raspberry gelatin
2 (16 oz.) cans whole berry
    cranberry sauce

2 C. unpeeled diced
    tart apple
1 C. chopped celery
½ C. chopped walnuts

Preparation

Spray a 9 x 13″ pan with nonstick cooking spray; set aside. In a medium bowl, combine gelatin and 2½ cups boiling water, stirring to dissolve. Stir in cranberry sauce until well mixed and refrigerate until gelatin just begins to congeal. Fold in apple, celery and walnuts. Pour into prepared pan. Return to refrigerator until set. Cut into squares to serve.

Garden Gelatin

makes 18 servings

Ingredients

2 (3 oz.) pkgs. lemon gelatin
2 tsp. distilled white vinegar
½ C. mayonnaise
1 C. grated carrots

1 C. chopped cabbage
1 onion, chopped
Salt and pepper to taste

Preparation

Spray a 9 x 13″ pan with nonstick cooking spray; set aside. In a large bowl, combine gelatin and 1¾ cups boiling water; stir to dissolve. Stir in 1¾ cups cold water and vinegar. Whisk in mayonnaise until well combined. Fold in carrots, cabbage and onion. Season with salt and pepper. Pour mixture into prepared pan and refrigerate until firm. Cut into squares to serve.

10-Layer Gelatin Salad

makes 18 servings

Ingredients

2 (3 oz.) pkgs. lemon gelatin
2 (3 oz.) pkgs. lime gelatin
2 (3 oz.) pkgs. orange gelatin
2 (3 oz.) pkgs. strawberry gelatin

2 (3 oz.) pkgs. black cherry gelatin
3 (12 oz.) cans evaporated milk

Preparation

Spray a 9 x 13" baking pan with nonstick cooking spray; set aside. In a small bowl, dissolve 1 package lemon gelatin in ¾ cup boiling water. Stir in ¾ cup evaporated milk and mix well. Pour into prepared pan. Refrigerate until set but still slightly sticky. In a small bowl, dissolve remaining 1 package lemon gelatin in ¾ cup boiling water. Stir in ¾ cup cold water. Pour over first layer in pan. Refrigerate until set but still slightly sticky. Repeat layers using lime, orange, strawberry and black cherry gelatin and remaining evaporated milk. Refrigerate until completely set, then cut in squares.

36

Festive Pineapple Cream

makes 18 servings

Ingredients

1 (3 oz.) pkg. cherry gelatin
1 (3 oz.) pkg. lemon gelatin
2 (8 oz.) tubs soft
   cream cheese
20 regular marshmallows
1 (2.6 oz.) pkg. dry
   whipped topping mix

Milk and vanilla extract
   according to whipped
   topping package directions
½ C. chopped
   maraschino cherries
½ C. mixed nuts
1 (3 oz.) pkg. lime gelatin
1 (8 oz.) can crushed
   pineapple, drained

Preparation

Spray a 9 x 13″ baking pan with nonstick cooking spray; set aside. In a small bowl, stir together cherry gelatin and 1 cup boiling water until gelatin dissolves. Stir in 1 cup cold water. Pour into prepared pan and refrigerate until set. In a medium saucepan over medium heat, stir together lemon gelatin and 1 cup boiling water until gelatin dissolves. Stir in 1 cup cold water. Add cream cheese and marshmallows, stirring until melted and smooth; cool. In a small bowl, prepare whipped topping using milk and vanilla according to package directions. Add to cooled lemon mixture. Fold in maraschino cherries and nuts. When cherry gelatin has set, pour lemon mixture over cherry gelatin. Return to refrigerator until lemon mixture has set. In a medium bowl, stir together lime gelatin and 1 cup boiling water until gelatin dissolves. Stir in 1 cup cold water. Stir in pineapple. When lemon mixture has set, pour lime mixture over lemon mixture. Refrigerate overnight, then cut into squares to serve.

Red, White & Blue Salad

makes 18 servings

Ingredients

1 (3 oz.) pkg. blue gelatin
1 C. fresh blueberries
1 (.25 oz.) envelope
  unflavored gelatin
1 C. whipping cream
6 T. sugar
2 C. sour cream

1 tsp. vanilla extract
1 (3 oz.) pkg. raspberry gelatin
1 C. fresh raspberries
Whipped topping, thawed,
  and additional fresh berries
  for garnish, optional

Preparation

Spray a 9 x 13˝ baking pan with nonstick cooking spray; set aside. In a medium bowl, dissolve blue gelatin in 1 cup boiling water; stir in 1 cup cold water. Stir in blueberries. Pour mixture into prepared pan. Refrigerate for about 1 hour or until set. In a medium saucepan, sprinkle unflavored gelatin over ½ cup cold water; let stand for 1 minute. Add whipping cream and sugar; cook and stir over low heat until gelatin and sugar are completely dissolved. Cool to room temperature. Whisk in sour cream and vanilla. Pour sour cream mixture over blue gelatin layer. Refrigerate until set. In a medium bowl, dissolve raspberry gelatin in 1 cup boiling water; stir in 1 cup cold water. Stir in raspberries. Pour raspberry mixture over sour cream mixture. Refrigerate until set, then cut into squares to serve; garnish with whipped topping and fresh berries.

Side Dishes

Peachy Stuffing

makes 12 servings

Ingredients

1 (1 lb.) loaf Italian bread, cut into 1″ cubes
½ C. butter
1 onion, diced
4 celery stalks, chopped
4 tsp. minced garlic
Salt and pepper to taste
½ C. chopped fresh parsley
2 T. chopped fresh sage

2 tsp. chopped fresh thyme
1 (29 oz.) can peach halves in heavy syrup, cut into bite-size pieces, drained, syrup reserved
½ C. frozen orange juice concentrate, thawed
½ C. chicken stock

Preparation

Preheat oven to 300°. On a baking sheet, arrange bread in a single layer and bake for about 15 minutes until dry but not brown. Remove from oven and let cool. Increase oven temperature to 375° and spray a 9 x 13″ baking pan with nonstick cooking spray; set aside. In a large skillet over medium-high heat, melt butter. Add onion, celery and garlic, stirring to coat with butter. Season with salt and pepper. Cook, stirring occasionally, for 5 minutes or until softened. Stir in parsley, sage and thyme; cook for an additional 2 minutes. Transfer to a large bowl. Add bread cubes. Toss to combine. In a large bowl, whisk together reserved peach syrup and orange juice concentrate and stir into bread mixture. Stir in peach pieces and chicken stock. Transfer mixture to prepared pan and cover with parchment paper and aluminum foil. Bake for 25 minutes. Uncover and bake for 15 to 20 minutes more or until golden brown. Serve immediately.

Apricot Stuffing

makes 12 servings

Ingredients

2 T. olive oil

1 onion, chopped

4 leeks, dark green portion removed and discarded

4 C. chopped celery

4 garlic cloves, minced

8 oz. shiitake mushrooms, sliced

10 C. cubed white sandwich bread, crusts removed

2 C. dried apricots, chopped

¼ C. chopped fresh sage

2 T. fresh thyme

2 C. vegetable stock

1 C. melted butter

Salt and pepper to taste

Preparation

Preheat oven to 375°. Spray a 9 x 13″ baking pan with nonstick cooking spray; set aside. Heat olive oil in a large skillet over medium heat. Add onion, leeks, celery and garlic. Cook stirring occasionally until onion is tender, about 20 minutes. Add mushrooms. Cook until soft, about 5 minutes. Transfer mixture to a large bowl and let stand for 10 to 15 minutes or until cool. Add bread cubes, apricots, sage and thyme. Stir to combine. Add vegetable stock, butter, salt and pepper; toss. Transfer stuffing mixture to prepared pan. Bake for 50 to 55 minutes or until top is crisp and stuffing is heated through. Let stand for 10 minutes before serving.

Cheesy Mashed Potatoes

makes 10 to 12 servings

Ingredients

5 large baking potatoes
1 C. shredded Mexican cheese blend
½ C. chopped green onion
1 (8 oz.) container sour cream
1 (8 oz.) container cottage cheese
¼ C. melted butter
1 tsp. salt
½ tsp. pepper

Preparation

Preheat oven to 350°. Spray a 9 x 13″ baking pan with nonstick cooking spray; set aside. Wash, peel and dice potatoes. Cook in boiling water until tender; drain. Place potatoes in a large bowl and mash. Add cheese, onion, sour cream, cottage cheese, butter, salt and pepper; blend well. Transfer mixture to prepared pan and bake for 20 to 25 minutes or until top is light brown. Serve immediately.

Scalloped Dijon Potatoes

makes 10 to 12 servings

Ingredients

1 onion, chopped

2 (3 oz.) pkgs. cream cheese, softened

1 (14.5 oz.) can chicken broth

1 T. prepared Dijon mustard

1½ lbs. (about 5 C.) potatoes, peeled, thinly sliced

2 C. crushed butter-flavored crackers

3 T. grated Parmesan cheese

2 T. melted butter

2 T. chopped fresh parsley

Preparation

Preheat oven to 350°. Spray a 9 x 13″ baking pan with nonstick cooking spray; set aside. Spray a large skillet with nonstick cooking spray and heat over medium-high heat. Add onion; cook, stirring frequently, 5 to 7 minutes or until tender. Add cream cheese, chicken broth and mustard; mix well. Remove from heat. In a large bowl, toss together potatoes and cream cheese mixture; transfer to prepared pan. In a small bowl, combine crushed crackers, Parmesan cheese, butter and parsley; sprinkle over potatoes. Bake for 50 to 60 minutes or until potatoes are tender. Let stand for 5 minutes before serving.

Old-Fashioned Au Gratins

makes 10 to 12 servings

Ingredients

3 large baking potatoes, peeled, cubed

1 C. whipping cream

½ C. milk

4 cloves garlic, minced

2 T. flour

Salt and pepper to taste

1 C. shredded Cheddar cheese

Preparation

Preheat oven to 350°. Spray a 9 x 13" baking pan with nonstick cooking spray. Arrange potatoes evenly in prepared pan. In a small bowl, whisk together whipping cream, milk, garlic, flour, salt and pepper. Pour evenly over potatoes. Cover with aluminum foil and bake for 20 minutes. Remove foil and continue baking for 40 minutes or until potatoes are tender. Sprinkle with cheese and bake for an additional 5 to 10 minutes or until cheese is melted. Cool for 5 minutes before serving.

Ranch Spuds

Ingredients

½ C. bottled ranch dressing
½ C. shredded Italian
cheese blend
¼ C. bacon bits

2 lbs. (about 6 C.) small
red potatoes, quartered
1 T. chopped fresh parsley

Preparation

Preheat oven to 350°. Spray a 9 x 13″ baking pan with nonstick cooking spray; set aside. In a large bowl, mix together dressing, cheese and bacon bits; stir in potatoes. Transfer to prepared pan; cover with aluminum foil and bake for 40 minutes. Remove foil and bake for 15 minutes more or until potatoes are tender. Sprinkle with parsley before serving.

Tater Casserole

makes 10 to 12 servings

Ingredients

1 (2 lb.) pkg. frozen Southern-
style hash browns, thawed
1 (10.7 oz.) can cream
of chicken soup
1 (16 oz.) container
sour cream

½ C. melted butter
½ C. chopped onion
½ tsp. salt
½ tsp. pepper
2 C. shredded
Cheddar cheese

Preparation

Preheat oven to 350°. Spray a 9 x 13″ baking pan with nonstick cooking spray. Pour potatoes into prepared pan. In a medium bowl, stir together soup, sour cream, butter, onion, salt and pepper. Pour over potatoes. Sprinkle cheese over all. Bake for 1 hour. Serve immediately.

Sweet Potato Gratin

makes 10 to 12 servings

Ingredients

7 T. butter, divided

4 lbs. sweet potatoes, peeled, thinly sliced

1 (8 oz.) can crushed pineapple with juice

1 C. orange juice

½ C. brown sugar

1 tsp. ground ginger

⅛ tsp. ground nutmeg

Salt and white pepper to taste

Preparation

Preheat oven to 350°. Grease a 9 x 13″ baking pan using 1 tablespoon butter. Arrange half of the sweet potatoes in prepared pan. Cut remaining 6 tablespoons butter into small cubes and arrange half over sweet potatoes. In a small bowl, stir together pineapple with juice, orange juice, brown sugar, ginger, nutmeg, salt and pepper. Pour half of the mixture over sweet potatoes. Repeat layers. Bake for 40 to 45 minutes or until sweet potatoes are tender, basting with juices occasionally. If the top gets too brown, cover with aluminum foil and continue baking until sweet potatoes are tender. Serve immediately.

Cranberry & Orange Sweet Potatoes

makes 10 to 12 servings

Ingredients

2 C. fresh or frozen cranberries
¾ C. orange juice
⅓ C. chopped walnuts
½ C. brown sugar
½ tsp. salt

½ tsp. ground nutmeg
½ tsp. ground cinnamon
4 medium sweet potatoes,
   peeled, sliced, cooked

Preparation

Preheat oven to 350°. Spray a 9 x 13″ baking pan with nonstick cooking spray; set aside. In a large bowl, combine cranberries, orange juice, walnuts, brown sugar, salt, nutmeg and cinnamon. Add to cooked sweet potatoes; toss to coat. Transfer mixture to prepared pan, cover with aluminum foil and bake for 40 minutes or until heated through. Serve immediately.

Variation

To make *Squash & Apple Sweet Potatoes*, replace cranberries and walnuts with 1 small butternut squash, peeled, cubed and cooked and 1 baking apple, thinly sliced. Stir in ¼ cup honey and 1 cup dried apricots, cut into 1″ pieces. Assemble and bake as directed.

Yellow Squash & Zucchini Casserole

makes 12 servings

Ingredients

3 C. diced yellow squash
3 C. diced zucchini
1 T. vegetable oil
1 onion, chopped
¼ C. butter
½ C. sour cream

¾ tsp. salt
⅛ tsp. pepper
⅛ tsp. garlic powder
1 C. shredded Cheddar cheese
1 C. crushed butter-flavored crackers

Preparation

Preheat oven to 350°. Spray a 9 x 13″ baking pan with nonstick cooking spray; set aside. In a large skillet over medium heat, sauté squash and zucchini in vegetable oil for 15 to 20 minutes until very soft; drain completely. In a medium skillet, sauté the onion in butter for 5 minutes. Transfer to a large bowl. Stir in squash and zucchini. Add sour cream, salt, pepper, garlic powder and cheese. Transfer to prepared pan. Sprinkle with crushed crackers. Bake for 25 to 30 minutes. Serve immediately.

Creamy Squash Bake

makes 12 servings

Ingredients

½ C. butter, divided
1 (8 oz.) pkg. herb stuffing mix
3 lbs. yellow squash, sliced
¼ C. flour
1 C. milk
1 tsp. salt
½ tsp. pepper

Pinch of ground nutmeg
1½ C. shredded carrots
1 (8 oz.) container sour cream
1 (4 oz.) jar chopped
  pimientos
½ C. chopped onion

Preparation

Preheat oven to 350°. Spray a 9 x 13″ baking pan with nonstick cooking spray; set aside. In a large saucepan over medium heat, melt ¼ cup butter. Add stuffing mix and toss to coat evenly. Spread half of the stuffing in prepared pan. In a steamer basket set over simmering water, steam squash for 8 minutes or until tender; mash and drain. Meanwhile, in a large saucepan over medium heat, melt remaining ¼ cup butter. Stir in flour and cook for 1 minute. Gradually stir in milk. Bring to a boil. Cook for 1 minute, stirring constantly. Add salt, pepper and nutmeg. Remove from heat and stir in squash, carrots, sour cream, pimientos and onion. Pour squash mixture over stuffing in pan and spread remaining half of the stuffing over squash. Bake for 30 minutes or until hot and bubbly. Serve immediately.

Old-Time Green Bean Casserole

makes 10 to 12 servings

Ingredients

3 T. butter, divided
2 T. flour
1 tsp. salt
1 tsp. sugar
¼ C. chopped onion
1 C. sour cream

3 (14.5 oz.) cans French-style
   green beans, drained
2 C. shredded
   Cheddar cheese
½ C. crushed
   butter-flavored crackers

Preparation

Preheat oven to 350°. Spray a 9 x 13″ baking pan with nonstick cooking spray; set aside. In a large skillet over medium heat, melt 2 tablespoons butter. Stir in flour until smooth. Cook for 1 minute. Stir in salt, sugar, onion and sour cream. Add beans and stir to coat. Transfer mixture to prepared pan. Cover with cheese. In a small microwave-safe bowl, melt remaining 1 tablespoon butter in microwave. Add cracker crumbs and toss to coat. Sprinkle crumbs over cheese. Bake for 30 minutes or until golden and bubbly. Serve immediately.

Updated Green Bean Casserole

makes 10 to 12 servings

Ingredients

2 lbs. fresh green
 beans, trimmed
6 oz. fresh button mushrooms
1 sweet red bell
 pepper, chopped
3 T. olive oil, divided
2 T. balsamic vinegar
1 (3 oz.) pkg. cream cheese,
 softened, cubed

1 (4 oz.) pkg. goat cheese,
 softened, cubed
1 onion, cut in wedges
¼ C. brown sugar
½ C. dry bread crumbs
1 T. dried parsley flakes

Preparation

Preheat oven to 375°. Spray a 9 x 13˝ baking pan with nonstick cooking spray; set aside. In a medium saucepan over high heat, combine green beans and enough water to cover. Bring water to a boil and boil for 3 minutes; drain. Transfer beans to a large bowl; add mushrooms and bell pepper. In a small bowl, whisk together 2 tablespoons olive oil and vinegar. Pour over vegetable mixture and toss to coat. Transfer to prepared pan and bake for 15 minutes. Increase oven temperature to 400°. Add cream cheese and goat cheese; toss to coat and set aside. Meanwhile, in a small saucepan, sauté onion wedges in remaining 1 tablespoon olive oil and brown sugar until onion is just tender. Stir in bread crumbs and toss to coat. Arrange over warm vegetable mixture and bake an additional 5 to 8 minutes or until heated through. Sprinkle with parsley flakes before serving.

Jazzy Baked Beans

makes 12 to 18 servings

Ingredients

5 strips bacon, divided
4 (16 oz.) cans baked beans
1 (20 oz.) can crushed
   pineapple, drained
1 C. molasses

1 C. barbeque sauce
2 T. prepared yellow mustard
Salt and pepper to taste
1 (6 oz.) can French fried
   onions, divided

Preparation

Preheat oven to 350°. Spray a 9 x 13˝ baking pan with nonstick cooking spray; set aside. In a medium nonstick skillet over medium heat, fry bacon until crisp; drain and crumble. In a large bowl, mix together baked beans, pineapple, molasses, barbeque sauce, mustard, salt , pepper and half of the bacon and onions. Transfer mixture to prepared pan and sprinkle with remaining half of the bacon and onions. Bake for 1 hour or until beans are brown and bubbly. Serve warm.

Company Baked Beans

makes 12 to 18 servings

Ingredients

6 strips bacon
½ lb. ground beef
½ C. chopped onion
1 (53 oz.) can pork and beans
1 (16 oz.) can kidney beans, rinsed, drained
1 (15.5 oz.) can black-eyed peas, rinsed, drained

½ C. ketchup
⅓ C. sugar
⅓ C. brown sugar
⅓ C. barbeque sauce
2 T. molasses
2 T. prepared yellow mustard
½ tsp. chili powder
Salt and pepper to taste

Preparation

Preheat oven to 350°. Spray a 9 x 13" baking pan with nonstick cooking spray; set aside. In a large skillet, cook bacon until brown and crisp; drain and crumble. Meanwhile, in a large nonstick saucepan over medium heat, cook ground beef and onion until meat is no longer pink; drain. Return mixture to saucepan and add pork and beans, kidney beans, black-eyed peas, ketchup, bacon, sugar, brown sugar, barbeque sauce, molasses, mustard, chili powder, salt, pepper and cooked bacon. Stir to combine. Transfer to prepared pan. Cover with aluminum foil and bake for 1 hour or until heated through and thickened. Serve hot.

Broccoli-Cheese Casserole

makes 10 to 12 servings

Ingredients

2 (10 oz.) pkgs. frozen
   chopped broccoli,
   cooked and drained
1 C. mayonnaise
1 C. shredded sharp
   Cheddar cheese

1 (10.7 oz.) can cream
   of mushroom soup
2 eggs, lightly beaten
2 C. crushed butter-flavored
   crackers
2 T. melted butter

Preparation

Preheat oven to 350°. Spray a 9 x 13″ baking pan with nonstick cooking spray; set aside. In a large bowl, combine broccoli, mayonnaise, cheese, soup and eggs. Mix well. Transfer mixture to prepared pan. Top with crushed crackers and drizzle melted butter evenly over the top. Bake for 35 minutes or until browned. Serve warm.

Cheesy Cabbage

makes 10 to 12 servings

Ingredients

1 head cabbage,
  cored, chopped
1 (10.7 oz.) can cream
  of celery soup

Salt and pepper to taste
12 slices American cheese
40 butter-flavored crackers
½ C. melted butter

Preparation

Preheat oven to 350°. Spray a 9 x 13″ baking pan with nonstick cooking spray; set aside. In a large saucepan over high heat, bring 6 cups water to a boil. Reduce heat to medium, add cabbage and cook about 5 minutes or until crisp-tender; drain. Layer half of the cabbage, half of the soup, salt, pepper and six cheese slices in prepared pan. Repeat layers. Finely crush crackers. Stir together crackers and melted butter; sprinkle evenly over vegetable mixture. Bake for 30 minutes or until heated through. Serve immediately.

Variation

To make *Smothered Cheesy Cabbage*, eliminate soup and crackers and reduce butter to ¼ cup. Sauté ½ cup finely chopped sweet green bell pepper and ¼ cup finely chopped onion in butter until tender. Add ¼ cup flour, stirring constantly for 1 minute. Gradually add 2 cups milk and stir until thickened and bubbly. Layer and bake as directed, setting aside top layer of cheese for later use. Stir together ½ cup mayonnaise and 3 tablespoons chili sauce; pour over baked cabbage, add remaining cheese and bake for 5 minutes more or until cheese melts.

Creamy Corn Casserole

makes 10 to 12 servings

Ingredients

½ C. melted butter

1 C. sour cream

1 (15.2 oz.) can
whole-kernel corn

1 (14.7 oz.) can
cream-style corn

1 (8.5 oz.) pkg. corn
muffin mix

Preparation

Preheat oven to 350°. Spray a 9 x 13″ baking pan with nonstick cooking spray; set aside. In a medium bowl, stir together melted butter, sour cream, whole-kernel corn, cream-style corn and muffin mix. Pour into prepared pan. Bake for 45 to 60 minutes or until heated through.

Chilly Vegetable Pizza

makes 12 servings

Ingredients

1 (8 oz.) tube refrigerated crescent rolls

1 (8 oz.) pkg. cream cheese, softened

⅓ C. mayonnaise

2 T. thinly sliced green onion

½ tsp. dried dillweed

½ C. shredded lettuce

⅓ C. sliced pitted ripe olives

¼ C. chopped sweet green bell pepper

¼ C. chopped cucumber

1 tomato, chopped

⅔ C. crumbled garlic-and-herb-flavored feta cheese

Preparation

Preheat oven to 375°. Spray a 9 x 13″ baking pan with nonstick cooking spray. Unroll crescent rolls and press onto bottom and 2″ up sides of prepared pan, pressing to seal seams. Bake for 8 to 10 minutes or until light brown; cool. In a medium bowl, combine cream cheese, mayonnaise, onion and dillweed. Spread mixture over cooled crust. Top with lettuce, olives, bell pepper, cucumber and tomato. Sprinkle with cheese. Cover and chill 2 to 4 hours before cutting and serving.

Cream-Filled Phyllo Dough

makes 12 servings

Ingredients

6 eggs
½ C. flour
1 tsp. salt
1 (24 oz.) container
   cottage cheese

1 (8 oz.) container sour cream
1 (16 oz.) pkg. phyllo
   dough, thawed
1 C. melted butter, divided

Preparation

Preheat oven to 325°. Spray a 9 x 13″ baking pan with nonstick cooking spray; set aside. In a large bowl, beat eggs. Add flour and salt; mix well. Stir in cottage cheese and sour cream; mix until well combined. Place two phyllo sheets in prepared pan. Brush with 2 tablespoons butter. Spread about ⅓ cup cheese mixture over dough. Repeat layers two times, ending with an additional layer of phyllo dough and drizzling any remaining butter over all. Bake for 1 hour or until golden brown. Cut into squares and serve warm.

Tomato & Brie Focaccia

makes 12 servings

Ingredients

2½ to 3 C. flour
2 (.25 oz.) pkgs. quick-rise yeast
1 tsp. sugar
1 tsp. salt
¼ C. plus 1 T. olive oil

1 (14.5 oz.) can diced tomatoes, drained
1 clove garlic, minced
1½ tsp. Italian seasoning
6 oz. Brie cheese, cubed

Preparation

Spray a 9 x 13″ baking pan with nonstick cooking spray; set aside. In a large bowl, combine 2 cups flour, yeast, sugar and salt. In a small saucepan over medium heat, heat 1 cup water and ¼ cup olive oil to 120° to130°. Add mixture to dry ingredients, beating until just moistened. Stir in enough remaining ½ to 1 cup flour to form soft dough. Turn dough onto lightly floured surface; knead for 6 to 8 minutes or until smooth and elastic. Place in a greased bowl, turning once to grease all sides. Cover and let rise for 20 minutes. Punch dough down and press in prepared pan. Cover and let rest for 10 minutes. In a small bowl, combine tomatoes, garlic, Italian seasoning and remaining 1 tablespoon olive oil. Spread mixture over dough; top with cheese. Bake for 25 to 30 minutes or until golden brown and cheese is melted. Cool on a wire rack before serving.

Oatmeal Shortbread

makes 12 servings

Ingredients

1½ C. oatmeal
¼ C. whole wheat flour
⅓ C. honey

⅓ C. vegetable oil
½ tsp. salt
1 tsp. vanilla extract

Preparation

Preheat oven to 325°. Grease and flour a 9 x 13" baking pan; set aside. In a large bowl, stir together oatmeal, flour, honey, oil, salt and vanilla until a stiff dough forms. Press mixture firmly in prepared pan. Bake for 30 minutes or until light brown. Cool for 10 minutes before cutting into squares and serving.

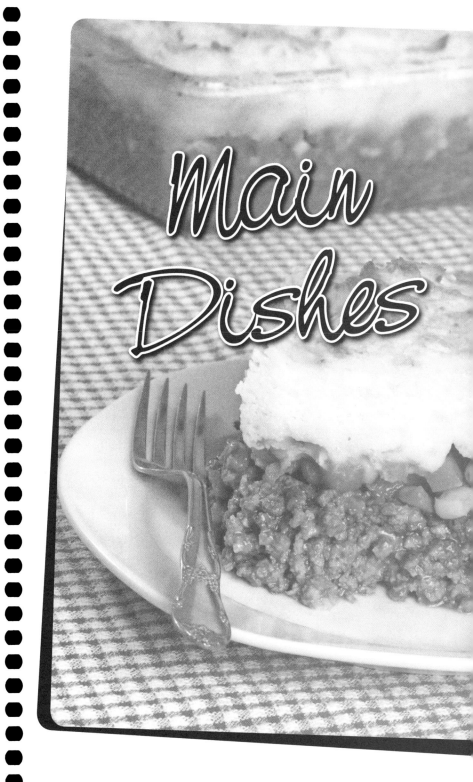

Main Dishes

Turkey Italiano

makes 6 servings

Ingredients

2 T. olive oil

6 turkey cutlets (about 1½ lbs.)

1 sweet green bell pepper,
   cut into strips

1 sweet red bell pepper,
   cut into strips

1 onion, sliced

1 (24 oz.) jar marinara sauce

1 C. shredded
   mozzarella cheese

1 (1 lb.) pkg. uncooked
   spaghetti

Preparation

Preheat oven to 450°. Spray a 9 x 13" baking pan with nonstick cooking spray; set aside. Heat olive oil in a large skillet over medium-high heat. Reduce heat to medium and sauté turkey for 3 to 4 minutes per side or until lightly browned. Remove turkey and set aside. To skillet, add green and red bell peppers and onion; sauté, stirring occasionally, for 8 minutes or until vegetables have softened. Spread ½ cup marinara sauce evenly in prepared pan. Arrange turkey cutlets over sauce, slightly overlapping if necessary. Pour 1 cup sauce evenly over turkey. Top with bell pepper mixture and sprinkle with cheese. Bake for 10 minutes or until cheese is melted. Meanwhile, in a large saucepan, cook spaghetti according to package directions until just tender; drain well. Toss spaghetti with remaining 1½ cups marinara sauce. Serve turkey mixture over spaghetti mixture.

Hearty Spinach & Chicken Manicotti

makes 6 servings

Ingredients

1 onion, chopped
1 clove garlic, minced
1 tsp. olive oil
2½ C. diced cooked chicken
1 (10 oz.) pkg. frozen chopped spinach, thawed, well drained
¾ C. diced ham
½ C. grated Parmesan cheese, divided

2 egg whites
½ tsp. dried basil
⅛ tsp. pepper
¾ C. flour
3 C. chicken broth
1 C. milk
¼ tsp. salt
⅛ tsp. cayenne pepper, optional
12 uncooked manicotti shells

Preparation

Preheat oven to 375°. Spray a 9 x 13″ baking pan with nonstick cooking spray; set aside. In a small skillet, sauté onion and garlic in olive oil until tender. In a large bowl, combine onion mixture, chicken, spinach, ham, ¼ cup Parmesan cheese, egg whites, basil and pepper. Stir to combine; set aside. In a large saucepan over medium heat, whisk together flour and chicken broth until smooth. Stir in milk, salt and cayenne pepper. Bring to a boil; cook and stir for 2 minutes or until thickened. Spoon 1 cup milk mixture into chicken mixture. Add remaining ¼ cup Parmesan cheese to remaining milk mixture; spread 1 cup in prepared pan. Cook manicotti shells according to package directions; drain. Stuff shells with chicken mixture. Arrange shells in pan. Drizzle evenly with remaining 3¾ cups milk mixture. Cover with aluminum foil and bake for 35 to 40 minutes or until bubbly. Serve hot.

Zesty Chicken & Rice

makes 4 servings

Ingredients

⅔ C. uncooked rice

1⅓ C. French fried onions, divided

½ tsp. Italian seasoning

1¾ C. chicken stock

4 boneless, skinless chicken breast halves

⅓ C. bottled Italian dressing

1 (16 oz.) pkg. frozen vegetable combination (broccoli, carrot, water chestnut, sweet red bell pepper)

Preparation

Preheat oven to 400°. Spray a 9 x 13″ baking pan with nonstick cooking spray. In prepared pan, stir together rice, ⅔ cup French fried onions and Italian seasoning. Pour chicken stock over rice mixture, stir and arrange chicken on top. Pour dressing over chicken and cover pan with aluminum foil. Bake for 30 minutes. Arrange frozen vegetables around chicken, covering rice. Bake uncovered for 20 to 25 minutes or until chicken and rice are tender. Top with remaining ⅔ cup French fried onions and bake for 1 to 3 minutes more or until onions are golden brown. Serve hot.

Easy Chicken Broccoli Rice

makes 6 servings

Ingredients

2 C. milk
½ C. mayonnaise
½ tsp. dried thyme
½ tsp. garlic powder
2 C. uncooked instant
  brown rice
1¼ lb. boneless, skinless
  chicken breast halves,
  cut into bite-size pieces

1 (10 oz.) pkg. frozen chopped
  broccoli, thawed, drained
1½ C. shredded sharp
  Cheddar cheese

Preparation

Preheat oven to 350°. Spray a 9 x 13″ baking pan with nonstick
cooking spray. Mix milk, mayonnaise, thyme and garlic powder
in prepared pan. Stir in rice, chicken and broccoli. Bake for
30 minutes or until chicken is cooked through. Remove from
oven and sprinkle with cheese. Let stand 5 minutes or until
cheese is melted and liquid is absorbed. Serve hot.

Hot Chicken Salad

makes 8 to 12 servings

Ingredients

2 C. chopped cooked chicken
1 C. chopped celery
½ C. slivered almonds
½ tsp. salt
½ tsp. pepper

2 T. lemon juice
1 C. mayonnaise
1 C. shredded sharp
  Cheddar cheese
⅔ C. crushed potato chips

Preparation

Preheat oven to 350°. Spray a 9 x 13″ baking pan with nonstick cooking spray; set aside. In a large bowl, combine chicken, celery, almonds, salt, pepper, lemon juice, mayonnaise and Cheddar cheese. Transfer to prepared pan. Sprinkle with crushed potato chips. Bake for 20 minutes or until bubbly. Serve hot.

One Pot Tex-Mex Chicken Casserole

makes 8 to 12 servings

Ingredients

1 C. salsa
1 (14.5 oz.) can stewed
   tomatoes
1 (8 oz.) container plain yogurt
½ C. milk
¾ tsp. salt
1 (10 oz.) pkg. frozen corn,
   partially thawed
12 (6″) corn tortillas,
   torn into bite-size pieces
1 (6 oz.) can pitted ripe olives

1 (16 oz.) can black beans,
   rinsed, drained
1½ C. shredded
   cooked chicken
1 scallion, chopped
¼ C. chopped fresh cilantro
¼ tsp. pepper
1 tsp. ground cumin
1 tsp. dried oregano
1 C. shredded sharp
   Cheddar cheese

Preparation

Preheat oven to 350°. Spray a 9 x 13″ baking pan with nonstick cooking spray. Sprinkle ½ cup corn in prepared pan. Arrange half of the tortillas over the corn, overlapping if necessary. In a small bowl, stir together salsa and tomatoes. In another small bowl, stir together yogurt, milk and salt. Pour 1 cup salsa mixture and ½ cup yogurt mixture over tortillas; sprinkle with olives. Reserve ¼ cup each corn and beans; sprinkle remaining corn and beans in pan. Top with chicken, scallion, cilantro, pepper, cumin, oregano, ½ cup cheese and ½ cup salsa mixture. Layer remaining tortillas, reserved corn and beans, remaining 1 cup salsa mixture, 1 cup yogurt mixture and ½ cup cheese. Cover with aluminum foil and bake for 15 minutes. Uncover and bake for 10 minutes more or until light brown. Serve hot.

Mac & Cheese Chicken Casserole

makes 8 to 12 servings

Ingredients

1 C. chopped celery

1 C. chopped sweet green bell pepper

¾ C. chopped onion

2 T. butter, softened

1 C. chicken broth

2 C. frozen vegetable combination (peas, corn)

Salt and pepper to taste

3 C. cubed cooked chicken

½ (16 oz.) pkg. uncooked elbow macaroni, cooked, drained

1 (4 oz.) can sliced mushrooms, drained

1 C. shredded American cheese

Preparation

Preheat oven to 350°. Spray a 9 x 13″ baking pan with nonstick cooking spray; set aside. In a large skillet over medium heat, sauté celery, bell pepper and onion in butter until tender. Add chicken broth, frozen vegetables, salt and pepper. Cook until heated through. Stir in chicken and macaroni. Transfer mixture to prepared pan. Top with mushrooms and cheese. Cover with aluminum foil and bake for 20 minutes. Uncover and bake for 10 minutes more or until heated through. Serve warm.

Pasta & Kielbasa

makes 8 to 12 servings

Ingredients

1 (16 oz.) pkg. bow tie pasta
1 (10 oz.) pkg. frozen
  peas, thawed
1 lb. kielbasa, sliced ½" thick
2 (10.7 oz.) cans Cheddar
  cheese soup

2⅔ C. milk
1 tsp. hot pepper sauce
¼ tsp. pepper

Preparation

Preheat oven to 350°. Spray a 9 x 13" baking pan with nonstick cooking spray; set aside. Cook pasta according to package directions until al dente; drain well. Transfer to prepared pan. Pour peas evenly over pasta. In a medium skillet over medium-high heat, cook kielbasa for 5 to 7 minutes or until browned. Add to pasta and peas. In a medium bowl, whisk together soup, milk, hot pepper sauce and pepper. Pour over mixture in pan; toss to coat. Bake for 30 minutes or until heated through. Serve hot.

Spicy Sausage Manicotti

makes 6 servings

Ingredients

½ lb. bulk spicy Italian sausage
1 (15 oz.) can crushed
  tomatoes
1½ C. marinara sauce
1 egg, beaten
1½ C. ricotta cheese
⅓ C. grated Parmesan cheese
1 (4 oz.) can diced green chiles

1½ T. chopped fresh parsley
½ tsp. Italian seasoning
¼ tsp. salt
¼ tsp. garlic powder
¼ tsp. pepper
12 uncooked manicotti shells
¼ C. shredded
  mozzarella cheese

Preparation

Preheat oven to 375°. Spray a 9 x 13" baking pan with nonstick cooking spray; set aside. In a large skillet over medium heat, cook sausage until no longer pink; drain and set aside. In the same skillet, bring tomatoes and marinara sauce to a boil. Reduce heat, cover and simmer for 10 minutes. Pour 1 cup sauce mixture evenly into prepared pan. In a large bowl, combine egg, ricotta cheese, Parmesan cheese, chiles, parsley, Italian seasoning, salt, garlic powder and pepper. Stuff uncooked manicotti shells with cheese mixture. Place stuffed shells in prepared pan and cover evenly with sausage and remaining 2½ cups sauce. Cover with aluminum foil and bake for 50 minutes. Uncover, sprinkle with mozzarella cheese and bake for 10 minutes more or until cheese is melted and manicotti is tender. Let stand for 5 minutes before serving.

Rigatoni & Spicy Sausage

makes 8 to 12 servings

Ingredients

1 onion, sliced

1 T. olive oil

1 sweet red bell
pepper, chopped

3 cloves garlic, minced

½ tsp. fennel seed, crushed

1 lb. bulk spicy Italian sausage

2 (24 oz.) jars tomato
& basil pasta sauce

1 T. white wine vinegar

5 C. uncooked rigatoni pasta

2 C. shredded Italian
cheese blend

¼ C. grated Parmesan cheese

2 T. chopped fresh parsley

Preparation

Preheat oven to 400°. Spray a 9 x 13″ baking pan with nonstick cooking spray; set aside. In a heavy skillet over medium-high heat, sauté onion in olive oil for 5 minutes. Add bell pepper, garlic and fennel seed; reduce heat to medium and cook for 10 minutes or until onion is tender and golden brown. Transfer mixture to a large bowl. Cut sausage into 1″ pieces, add to skillet and cook for 8 minutes or until browned on all sides; drain. In skillet stir together sausage, pasta sauce, vinegar and. vegetable mixture. Reduce heat to medium-low; simmer for 15 minutes. Meanwhile, in a large saucepan, cook pasta according to package directions until al dente; drain, reserving 1 cup cooking water. In saucepan stir together pasta, sauce mixture and reserved cooking water. In a medium bowl, combine Italian cheese blend and Parmesan cheese. Stir 1¼ cups cheese mixture into pasta mixture and pour into prepared pan. Sprinkle with remaining cheese mixture and parsley. Bake covered for 30 to 45 minutes; uncover and bake for 15 minutes more or until golden brown. Serve hot.

Make-Ahead Ham Casserole

makes 10 to 12 servings

Ingredients

1 lb. ham, cubed
3 (15 oz.) cans Great Northern beans, drained, rinsed
1 onion, diced
1 Granny Smith apple, diced

3 T. molasses
3 T. brown sugar
1 T. prepared Dijon mustard
1 tsp. ground allspice
¼ C. sliced green onion

Preparation

Preheat oven to 350°. Spray a 9 x 13″ baking pan with nonstick cooking spray. In prepared pan, stir together ham, beans, onion, apple, molasses, brown sugar, mustard and allspice. Cover with aluminum foil and bake for 45 minutes or until liquid is absorbed. Cool; cover and refrigerate overnight.

Preheat oven to 350°. Stir ⅓ cup water into casserole. Bake for 40 minutes or until hot and bubbly. Sprinkle with green onion before serving.

Cheesy Ham & Hash Browns

makes 8 to 12 servings

Ingredients

1 (32 oz.) pkg. frozen shredded hash browns, thawed

8 oz. diced ham

2 (10.7 oz.) cans cream of potato soup

1 (16 oz.) container sour cream

2 C. shredded sharp Cheddar cheese

1½ C. grated Parmesan cheese

Preparation

Preheat oven to 375°. Spray a 9 x 13″ baking pan with nonstick cooking spray; set aside. In a large bowl, mix together hash browns, ham, soup, sour cream and Cheddar cheese. Spread evenly in prepared pan. Sprinkle with Parmesan cheese. Bake for 1 hour or until bubbly and golden brown. Serve immediately.

Variation

To make *Cheesy Ham & Hash Browns O'Brien*, replace shredded hash browns with Potatoes O'Brien, ham with bacon and 1 can cream of potato soup with cheddar cheese soup.

Creamy Pork Tenderloin

makes 8 servings

Ingredients

2 lbs. pork tenderloin
1 egg
½ tsp. dried rosemary, crushed
¼ tsp. pepper
⅛ tsp. garlic powder
1 C. seasoned dry bread crumbs

3 T. vegetable oil
2 T. butter
8 oz. fresh mushrooms, sliced
1 (10.7 oz.) can cream of mushroom soup
1 (8 oz.) container sour cream
¼ C. beef broth

Preparation

Preheat oven to 325°. Cut tenderloin into 16 pieces. Place each piece between two pieces of plastic wrap and flatten to ¾" thick. In a shallow dish, combine egg, 1 tablespoon water, rosemary, pepper and garlic powder; whisk until well combined. Put bread crumbs in another shallow dish. Heat vegetable oil in a large skillet over medium heat. Dip both sides of tenderloin pieces in egg mixture and then coat in bread crumbs. Place in hot oil and brown for 5 minutes on each side. Transfer to an ungreased 9 x 13" baking pan. Add butter to skillet and sauté mushrooms until tender. Stir in soup, sour cream and beef broth. Pour mixture evenly over tenderloin pieces in pan. Cover with aluminum foil and bake for 1 hour. Serve immediately.

Pork Chops & Stuffing

makes 6 servings

Ingredients

6 (¾" thick) boneless
  pork loin chops
Salt and pepper to taste
1 T. vegetable oil
1 onion, chopped
2 stalks celery, chopped
2 apples*, peeled, chopped

1 (14.5 oz.) can chicken
  broth
1 (10.7 oz.) can cream
  of celery soup
¼ C. dry white wine
6 C. herb-seasoned
  stuffing mix

Preparation

Preheat oven to 375°. Spray a 9 x 13" baking pan with nonstick cooking spray; set aside. Season pork chops with salt and pepper. Heat vegetable oil in a large skillet over medium-high heat. Add pork chops and cook until browned on both sides, turning once. Remove from skillet and set aside. Add onion and celery to skillet and cook, stirring occasionally, for 3 minutes or until onion is tender. Add apples; cook and stir for 1 minute. Add chicken broth, soup and wine; mix well. Bring to a simmer; remove from heat. Stir in stuffing mix until well combined. Spread stuffing mixture evenly in prepared pan. Place pork chops on top of stuffing and pour juices from pan over pork chops. Cover with aluminum foil and bake for 30 to 40 minutes or until pork chops are done. Serve immediately.

Tart apples such as Granny Smith work best.

Baked Beef Stew

makes 8 to 10 servings

Ingredients

2 lbs. beef stew meat, cut into 1″ pieces
6 carrots, sliced
3 potatoes, peeled, quartered
1 onion, sliced

½ C. sliced celery
1 (14.5 oz.) can diced tomatoes
3 T. quick-cooking tapioca
½ C. soft bread crumbs

Preparation

Preheat oven to 325°. Spray a 9 x 13″ baking pan with nonstick cooking spray; set aside. In a large bowl, stir together stew meat, carrots, potatoes, onion, celery, tomatoes, tapioca and bread crumbs. Transfer mixture to prepared pan. Cover with aluminum foil and bake for 3½ hours or until meat is tender. Serve hot.

Meat & Potato Bake

makes 10 to 12 servings

Ingredients

4 C. thinly sliced potatoes
2 T. melted butter
½ tsp. salt
1 lb. ground beef
1 (10 oz.) pkg. frozen corn
1 (10.7 oz.) can cream
   of celery soup

⅓ C. milk
¼ tsp. garlic powder
⅛ tsp. pepper
1 T. chopped onion
1 C. shredded Cheddar
   cheese, divided
Minced fresh parsley, optional

Preparation

Preheat oven to 400°. Spray a 9 x 13″ baking pan with nonstick cooking spray; set aside. In a medium bowl, toss together potatoes, butter and salt. Arrange potato slices along the bottom and up the sides of prepared pan. Bake for 25 to 30 minutes or until potatoes are almost tender. Meanwhile, in a large skillet over medium heat, cook and crumble ground beef until meat is no longer pink; drain. Transfer beef to potato-lined pan. Cover evenly with corn. In a small bowl, whisk together soup, milk, garlic powder, pepper, onion and ½ cup cheese; pour evenly over beef mixture. Bake for 20 minutes or until vegetables are tender. Remove from oven and sprinkle with remaining ½ cup cheese. Bake for 2 to 3 minutes more or until cheese is melted. Serve immediately.

Shepherd's Pie

makes 8 to 10 servings

Ingredients

2½ lbs. potatoes, peeled, cooked

1 (8 oz.) container sour cream

Salt and pepper to taste

2 lbs. ground beef

1 sweet red bell pepper, chopped

½ C. chopped onion

1 (15.2 oz.) can whole-kernel corn, drained

1 (10.7 oz.) can cream of mushroom soup

½ C. milk

1 tsp. garlic salt

2 T. melted butter

Chopped fresh parsley

Preparation

Preheat oven to 350°. In a large bowl, mash potatoes with sour cream. Add salt and pepper; set aside. In a large skillet, cook ground beef, bell pepper and onion until meat is no longer pink and vegetables are tender; drain. Add corn, soup, milk and garlic salt; mix well. Transfer meat mixture to an ungreased 9 x 13" baking pan. Top with mashed potato mixture; drizzle with butter. Bake for 30 to 35 minutes or until heated through. Sprinkle with parsley before serving.

Beef Enchiladas

makes 6 servings

Ingredients

¾ lb. ground beef
1 onion, chopped
1 clove garlic, minced
2 T. olive oil
1 (4 oz.) can diced green chiles
2 T. chili powder
¾ tsp. salt
12 (6″) corn tortillas

1½ C. refried beans
1 C. picante sauce
¼ C. shredded Cheddar
   cheese
2 T. sour cream, optional
1 tomato, chopped, optional
Chopped fresh cilantro,
   optional

Preparation

Preheat oven to 400°. Spray a 9 x 13″ baking pan with nonstick cooking spray; set aside. In a large skillet over medium-high heat, cook ground beef, onion and garlic in olive oil for 3 to 4 minutes or until beef is no longer pink. Stir in chiles, chili powder, salt and ¼ cup water. Bring to boiling; cook, stirring occasionally, for 10 minutes. Remove from heat. Warm tortillas according to package directions. Spread 2 tablespoons refried beans on a warm tortilla. Fill with about ¼ cup meat mixture. Roll up and place seam side down in prepared pan. Repeat with remaining 11 tortillas, refried beans and meat mixture. Spread picante sauce evenly over tortillas. Sprinkle with Cheddar cheese. Bake for 15 to 20 minutes or until cheese is melted and filling is hot. Serve with sour cream, tomato and cilantro, if desired.

Cheesy Spaghetti Bake

makes 12 servings

Ingredients

½ lb. uncooked spaghetti, broken into 3″ pieces
2 lbs. ground beef
1 onion, chopped
1 sweet green bell pepper, chopped

2 C. milk
2 (10.7 oz.) cans tomato soup
1 (10.7 oz.) can cream of mushroom soup
2 C. shredded sharp Cheddar cheese, divided

Preparation

Preheat oven to 350°. Spray a 9 x 13″ baking pan with nonstick cooking spray; set aside. Cook spaghetti according to package directions; drain. Spread spaghetti evenly in prepared pan; set aside. In a large saucepan over medium heat, cook ground beef, onion and bell pepper until meat is no longer pink and vegetables are tender; drain and return to pan. Add milk, tomato soup, cream of mushroom soup and 1 cup cheese. Bring to a boil. Pour over spaghetti in pan. Sprinkle with remaining 1 cup cheese. Bake for 40 to 45 minutes or until bubbly and light brown. Serve hot.

Mexican Lasagna

makes 12 servings

Ingredients

12 uncooked lasagna noodles
1 lb. ground beef
1 (16 oz.) can refried beans
1 (1 oz.) pkg. taco
  seasoning mix
1 clove garlic, minced
2½ C. salsa

1 C. shredded Pepper
  Jack cheese
¾ C. chopped green onion
1 (2.25 oz.) can sliced pitted
  ripe olives
1 tomato, chopped
2 C. sour cream

Preparation

Preheat oven to 350°. Spray a 9 x 13″ baking pan with nonstick cooking spray. Line prepared pan with four uncooked lasagna noodles; set aside. In a large skillet over medium heat, cook ground beef until no longer pink; drain. In a large bowl, stir together ground beef, refried beans, seasoning mix and garlic. Spread half of the mixture over noodles in pan. Top with four more noodles and remaining half of the beef mixture. Cover with remaining four noodles. In a medium bowl, stir together salsa and 2½ cups water; pour over noodles in pan. Cover tightly with aluminum foil and bake for 1½ hours or until noodles are tender; sprinkle with cheese. Return to oven and bake uncovered for an additional 5 to 10 minutes or until cheese melts. Remove from oven and sprinkle with onion, olives and tomato. Let stand for 10 minutes. Add dollops of sour cream before serving.

Fiesta Casserole

makes 8 to 10 servings

Ingredients

1 lb. ground beef

1 sweet green bell pepper, chopped

1 sweet red bell pepper, chopped

1 (16 oz.) jar salsa

1 (14.5 oz.) can diced tomatoes with juice

1 (10 oz.) pkg. frozen corn, thawed

12 (6˝) flour tortillas

1½ C. sharp Cheddar cheese, divided

Preparation

Preheat oven to 375°. Spray a 9 x 13˝ baking pan with nonstick cooking spray; set aside. In a large skillet over medium heat, cook ground beef and green and red bell peppers until meat is no longer pink and vegetables are tender; drain. Stir in salsa, tomatoes and corn; bring to a boil. Spoon 1 cup meat mixture into prepared pan. Top with half of the tortillas, overlapping if necessary. Spoon half of the remaining meat mixture over tortillas and sprinkle with ¾ cup cheese. Top with remaining six tortillas and remaining meat mixture. Cover with aluminum foil and bake for 25 to 30 minutes or until heated through. Remove from oven and sprinkle with remaining ¾ cup cheese. Let stand uncovered until cheese melts. Serve hot.

Zesty Seafood Lasagna

makes 8 to 10 servings

Ingredients

4 (.9 oz.) pkgs. béarnaise
  sauce mix
4½ C. milk
1 tsp. dried basil
½ tsp. dried thyme
½ tsp. garlic powder
¾ C. grated Parmesan
  cheese, divided
3 T. hot pepper sauce

9 oven-ready lasagna noodles
2 (10 oz.) pkgs. frozen
  chopped spinach,
  thawed, well drained
½ lb. cooked shrimp
½ lb. flaked imitation
  crabmeat
2 C. shredded mozzarella
  cheese, divided

Preparation

Preheat oven to 400°. Spray a 9 x 13″ baking pan with nonstick cooking spray; set aside. In a large saucepan, prepare béarnaise sauce according to package directions using milk and adding basil, thyme and garlic powder. Stir in Parmesan cheese and hot pepper sauce. Spread 1 cup sauce in prepared pan. Arrange three lasagna noodles side by side over sauce. Cover with half of the spinach, half of the shrimp and half of the crabmeat. Spread with 1 cup sauce and sprinkle with ¾ cup mozzarella cheese. Repeat lasagna noodle, spinach, shrimp and crabmeat layers. Top with remaining three lasagna noodles, remaining sauce and remaining 1¼ cups mozzarella cheese. Cover with aluminum foil sprayed with nonstick cooking spray. Bake for 40 minutes; remove foil and bake 10 minutes more until lasagna noodles are tender. Let stand for 15 minutes before serving.

Tuna Noodle Casserole

makes 10 to 12 servings

Ingredients

1 (12 oz.) pkg. uncooked wide egg noodles

¼ C. chopped onion

2 C. shredded Cheddar cheese, divided

1 C. frozen peas

1 (12 oz.) can tuna, drained

1 (10.7 oz.) can cream of mushroom soup

1 (10.7 oz.) can cream of celery soup

1 (4 oz.) can sliced mushrooms

1 C. crushed potato chips

Preparation

Preheat oven to 425°. Spray a 9 x 13″ baking pan with nonstick cooking spray; set aside. Cook pasta according to package directions until al dente; drain. In a large bowl, mix together cooked noodles, onion, 1 cup cheese, peas, tuna, cream of mushroom and cream of celery soups and mushrooms. Transfer mixture to prepared pan; top with potato chips and remaining 1 cup cheese. Bake for 15 to 20 minutes or until bubbly. Serve immediately.

Swiss Tuna Bake

makes 8 to 10 servings

Ingredients

1 (12 oz.) can tuna, drained
2 C. multigrain flake cereal,
  such as Wheaties
¼ C. dried minced onion
1 (10.7 oz.) can cream
  of onion soup

2 T. olive oil
1½ C. shredded Swiss cheese
½ C. dry roasted peanuts

Preparation

Preheat oven to 325°. Spray a 9 x 13″ baking pan with nonstick cooking spray; set aside. In a medium bowl, stir together tuna, cereal, onion, soup and olive oil. Transfer mixture to prepared pan. Sprinkle evenly with cheese and peanuts. Bake for 30 minutes or until bubbly. Cut into squares to serve.

Quick Baked Fish with Spinach

makes 6 servings

Ingredients

½ (16 oz.) pkg. uncooked
   egg noodles
3 T. butter
3 T. flour
3 C. milk
1½ C. shredded Cheddar
   cheese, divided
1 T. lemon juice
1 tsp. salt
1 tsp. dry mustard

1 tsp. Worcestershire sauce
⅛ tsp. ground nutmeg
⅛ tsp. pepper
2 (10 oz.) pkgs. frozen
   chopped spinach,
   thawed, well drained
1½ lbs. sole, halibut or
   flounder fillets
¼ C. slivered almonds,
   toasted*

Preparation

Preheat oven to 375°. Spray a 9 x 13″ baking pan with nonstick cooking spray; set aside. Cook noodles according to package directions; drain. Meanwhile, in a large saucepan, melt butter. Stir in flour and cook until smooth; gradually add milk, stirring constantly until the mixture boils. Cook and stir for 2 minutes or until thickened. Stir in 1 cup cheese, lemon juice, salt, dry mustard, Worcestershire sauce, nutmeg and pepper until cheese melts. Set aside half of the cheese sauce. Add noodles to remaining half of the cheese sauce. Stir to coat thoroughly. Transfer to prepared pan. Top with spinach, fish fillets, reserved cheese sauce and remaining ½ cup cheese. Sprinkle with almonds. Bake for 30 to 35 minutes or until fish flakes easily with a fork. Serve immediately.

* To toast, place almonds in a dry skillet over medium heat and cook until browned, about 3 to 5 minutes, shaking pan often.

Meatless Main Dishes

Cannelloni & Spinach

makes 4 to 6 servings

Ingredients

8 cannelloni or
  manicotti shells
1 T. butter
¼ C. chopped shallot,
  leek or green onion
1 (10 oz.) pkg. frozen
  chopped spinach,
  thawed, well drained

5 eggs, divided
5 oz. Havarti cheese,
  shredded, divided
¾ C. chopped fresh basil
3 tsp. salt, divided
¾ C. milk

Preparation

Preheat oven to 350°. Spray a 9 x 13″ baking pan with nonstick cooking spray; set aside. Cook cannelloni shells according to package directions. Drain and set aside. In a large skillet, melt butter and sauté shallot for 1 minute. Add spinach; cook and stir for 3 minutes. Remove from heat. In a large bowl, beat 3 eggs. Stir in half of the cheese. Add basil and 1½ teaspoons salt. Mix well. Add spinach mixture, stirring until well combined. Fill cooked shells with spinach mixture and place in a single layer in prepared pan. In a small bowl, whisk together milk, remaining 2 eggs and remaining 1½ teaspoons salt. Pour over stuffed shells. Bake for 30 minutes. Remove from oven and let stand for 10 minutes. Sprinkle with remaining half of the cheese before serving.

Sun-Dried Tomato Manicotti

makes 6 to 8 servings

Ingredients

1½ oz. (about 15 halves)
   sun-dried tomatoes
6 oven-ready lasagna sheets
1 (16 oz.) container
   ricotta cheese
2 T. chopped fresh parsley

¼ C. chopped fresh basil
1 egg yolk
1 tsp. salt
¼ tsp. pepper
1½ C. tomato sauce
3 T. grated Parmesan cheese

Preparation

Preheat oven to 450°. In a small bowl, cover tomatoes with
1 cup boiling water. Let stand about 15 minutes or until
softened. Dry and chop tomatoes. Transfer to a medium bowl;
set aside. Fill 9 x 13″ baking pan with very hot water; place
manicotti sheets one at a time in water and let stand for
10 minutes or until softened. Dry baking pan and spray with
nonstick cooking spray; set aside. Add ricotta cheese, parsley,
basil, egg yolk, salt and pepper to tomatoes in bowl. Mix well.
Spoon about ⅓ cup cheese mixture along one edge of each
manicotti sheet; roll up. Repeat. Pour ¼ cup tomato sauce
into prepared pan. Transfer manicotti to pan and cover with
remaining 1¼ cups tomato sauce; sprinkle with Parmesan
cheese. Cover with aluminum foil and bake for 10 minutes.
Remove foil and bake for 12 to 15 minutes more or until bubbly.

Primavera Lasagna

makes 8 to 10 servings

Ingredients

12 uncooked lasagna noodles
3 C. frozen broccoli, thawed, drained
2 C. shredded carrot
2 C. chopped tomato, drained
2 sweet red bell peppers, chopped
1 (15 oz.) container ricotta cheese

½ C. grated Parmesan cheese
1 egg
2 (10 oz.) containers refrigerated Alfredo pasta sauce
1 (16 oz.) pkg. shredded mozzarella cheese

Preparation

Preheat oven to 350°. Spray a 9 x 13″ baking pan with nonstick cooking spray; set aside. Cook noodles according to package directions; drain. Cut broccoli into bite-size pieces if necessary. In a large bowl, combine broccoli, carrot, tomato and bell peppers; stir. In a small bowl, stir together ricotta cheese, Parmesan cheese and egg. Mix well. Spread ⅔ cup Alfredo sauce in prepared pan. Top with four noodles, half of the cheese mixture and 2½ cups vegetables. Pour ⅔ cup sauce over vegetables. Sprinkle with 1 cup mozzarella cheese. Repeat noodle, cheese and vegetable layers. Pour ⅔ cup sauce over vegetables. Sprinkle with 1 cup mozzarella cheese. Top with remaining four noodles, 3 cups vegetables, ½ cup sauce and 2 cups mozzarella cheese. Bake for 45 to 60 minutes or until cooked through. Let stand for 15 minutes before cutting and serving.

Cheesy Spinach Lasagna

makes 8 to 10 servings

Ingredients

3 C. cottage cheese

3 eggs

Salt, pepper and garlic powder to taste

9 uncooked lasagna noodles

1 lb. shredded Monterey Jack cheese

1½ C. grated Parmesan cheese

3 (10 oz.) pkgs. frozen chopped spinach, thawed, well drained

¼ C. butter, melted

Preparation

Preheat oven to 350°. Spray a 9 x 13" baking pan with nonstick cooking spray; set aside. In a medium bowl, stir together cottage cheese, eggs, salt, pepper and garlic powder. In prepared pan, layer three lasagna noodles, ⅓ of the cottage cheese mixture, ⅓ of the Monterey Jack and Parmesan cheeses and ⅓ of the spinach. Repeat layers twice. Drizzle with melted butter. Bake for 30 to 40 minutes. Let stand for 10 minutes before serving.

Cheesy Baked Barley

makes 6 to 8 servings

Ingredients

¼ C. butter
¼ C. flour
2 C. warm milk
Salt and pepper to taste
2½ C. grated Parmesan cheese
1 C. grated Gruyère cheese

½ C. grated fontina cheese
6 C. chicken broth
2 C. barley, rinsed, drained
1 tsp. chopped fresh thyme
½ C. dry bread crumbs
Olive oil for drizzling

Preparation

Preheat oven to 400°. Spray a 9 x 13″ baking pan with nonstick cooking spray; set aside. In a medium saucepan over medium heat, melt butter. Add flour and whisk until smooth. Gradually add milk, whisking until sauce is thickened and smooth. Do not boil. Remove from heat and season with salt and pepper. In a large bowl, stir together Parmesan, Gruyère and fontina cheeses. Remove ½ cup cheese mixture and reserve. In a large saucepan over medium-high heat, bring chicken broth to a boil. Add barley and reduce heat to low. Simmer, stirring occasionally, for about 25 minutes or until barley is tender. Drain if necessary. Add barley, thyme and flour mixture to the cheese mixture in the large bowl. Stir to combine; season with salt and pepper. Pour the cheese mixture in prepared pan and top with reserved cheese. Sprinkle with bread crumbs and drizzle with olive oil. Bake for 25 to 30 minutes or until the top is golden brown. Let stand for 5 minutes before serving.

Baked Orzo & Veggies

makes 6 servings

Ingredients

4 C. hot cooked orzo or rosamarina pasta
3 eggs, beaten
2 T. soft bread crumbs
1 T. grated Parmesan cheese
1 T. basil pesto
¼ tsp. pepper

1 C. chopped tomato
1 (10 oz.) pkg. frozen chopped spinach, thawed, well drained
1 clove garlic, finely chopped
1 (15 oz.) can garbanzo beans, drained, rinsed

Preparation

Preheat oven to 350°. Spray a 9 x 13″ baking pan with nonstick cooking spray; set aside. In a large bowl, combine orzo, eggs, bread crumbs, cheese, pesto, pepper, tomato, spinach, garlic and beans. Pour in prepared pan. Bake for 30 minutes or until golden brown. Serve immediately.

Favorite Mac & Cheese

makes 8 to 10 servings

Ingredients

½ (16 oz.) pkg. uncooked elbow macaroni

1 (8 oz.) pkg. shredded sharp Cheddar cheese

1 (12 oz.) container cottage cheese

1 (8 oz.) container sour cream

¼ C. grated Parmesan cheese

Salt and pepper to taste

1 C. dry bread crumbs

¼ C. melted butter

Preparation

Preheat oven to 350°. Spray a 9 x 13″ baking pan with nonstick cooking spray; set aside. Cook macaroni according to package directions; drain. In a large bowl, stir together macaroni, Cheddar cheese, cottage cheese, sour cream, Parmesan cheese, salt and pepper. Transfer mixture to prepared pan. In a small bowl, mix together bread crumbs and butter. Sprinkle over macaroni mixture. Bake for 30 to 35 minutes or until top is golden brown. Serve hot.

Spinach & Feta "Pie"

makes 8 to 10 servings

Ingredients

⅓ C. melted butter, divided

2 eggs

1 (10 oz.) pkg. frozen chopped spinach, thawed, well drained

1 (15 oz.) container ricotta cheese

4 oz. crumbled feta cheese

½ tsp. grated lemon peel

¼ tsp. pepper

⅛ tsp. ground nutmeg

8 (13 x 18″) sheets phyllo dough (from a 16 oz. pkg.), thawed

Preparation

Preheat oven to 350°. Brush a 9 x 13″ baking pan lightly with a little melted butter; set aside. In a medium bowl, beat eggs. Stir in spinach, ricotta cheese, feta cheese, lemon peel, pepper and nutmeg; set aside. Unwrap phyllo dough and cut in half crosswise forming 16 (9 x 13″) rectangles. Cover with a damp cloth to keep moist. Place one dough rectangle in prepared pan; brush lightly with melted butter. Continue layering dough and melted butter until half of the dough has been used. Spread spinach mixture evenly over dough in pan. Top spinach mixture with one dough rectangle; brush lightly with melted butter. Continue layering dough and melted butter until remaining half of the dough has been used. Bake for 35 to 40 minutes or until golden brown. Let stand for 10 minutes before serving.

Cheesy Three-Vegetable Lasagna

makes 12 servings

Ingredients

8 oz. uncooked
    lasagna noodles
2 eggs, beaten
2 C. cottage cheese
1 (15 oz.) container
    ricotta cheese
2 tsp. Italian seasoning,
    crushed
2 T. olive oil
2 C. sliced fresh mushrooms
1 C. chopped onion
4 cloves garlic, minced

2 T. flour
½ tsp. pepper
1¼ C. milk
1 (10 oz.) pkg. frozen
    chopped spinach,
    thawed, well drained
1 (10 oz.) pkg. frozen chopped
    broccoli, thawed, drained
1 C. shredded carrot
¾ C. grated Parmesan cheese
1 (8 oz.) pkg. shredded
    mozzarella cheese

Preparation

Preheat oven to 350°. Spray a 9 x 13″ baking pan with nonstick cooking spray; set aside. Cook lasagna noodles according to package directions; drain and set aside. In a medium bowl, combine eggs, cottage cheese, ricotta cheese and Italian seasoning; set aside. Heat olive oil in a large skillet over medium heat. Add mushrooms, onion and garlic. Cook and stir until tender. Stir in flour and pepper; gradually add milk. Cook and stir until slightly thickened and bubbly. Remove from heat. Stir in spinach, broccoli, carrot and ½ cup Parmesan cheese. Layer ⅓ of the noodles in prepared pan, overlapping or cutting to fit. Spread with ⅓ of the cottage cheese mixture and ⅓ of the vegetable mixture. Sprinkle with ⅓ of the mozzarella cheese. Repeat layers twice. Sprinkle with remaining ¼ cup Parmesan cheese. Bake for 35 minutes or until heated through. Let stand for 10 minutes before serving.

Speedy Ravioli Lasagna

makes 8 to 10 servings

Ingredients

1 (8 oz.) can tomato sauce
1 (20 oz.) pkg. cheese ravioli
1 (24 oz.) jar marinara sauce
2 C. cottage cheese
2 eggs

¼ C. grated Parmesan cheese
1 tsp. dried oregano
2 C. shredded Italian cheese
 blend

Preparation

Preheat oven to 350°. Spray a 9 x 13" baking pan with nonstick cooking spray. Spread tomato sauce in prepared pan. Arrange half of the ravioli in a single layer over sauce. Pour half of the marinara sauce over ravioli. In a medium bowl, combine cottage cheese, eggs, Parmesan cheese and oregano; mix well. Carefully spread over sauce. Top with remaining half of the ravioli. Spread remaining half of the sauce over all. Bake for 40 to 50 minutes or until bubbly. Sprinkle with Italian cheese blend and bake an additional 3 minutes or until cheese melts. Let stand for 10 minutes before serving.

Baked Risotto

makes 6 to 8 servings

Ingredients

1 (28 oz.) jar spaghetti sauce
1 (14 oz.) can chicken broth
2 C. sliced zucchini
1 (4 oz.) can sliced mushrooms

1 C. short-grain rice
2 C. shredded
   mozzarella cheese

Preparation

Preheat oven to 350°. Spray a 9 x 13″ baking pan with nonstick cooking spray; set aside. In a medium bowl, combine spaghetti sauce, chicken broth, zucchini, mushrooms and rice. Stir to combine and transfer to prepared pan. Cover with aluminum foil and bake for 30 minutes. Remove from oven and stir. Cover and bake for 15 to 20 minutes more or until rice is tender. Remove from oven and sprinkle with cheese. Bake uncovered for 5 minutes or until cheese is melted. Serve hot.

Tomato & Eggplant Casserole

makes 6 to 8 servings

Ingredients

1 (1 lb.) eggplant, peeled, cut into ½" slices
Salt to taste
1 tomato, sliced
1 onion, sliced
6 T. melted butter, divided

½ tsp. dried basil
4 (.6 oz.) slices provolone cheese, each cut into thirds
½ C. dry bread crumbs
2 T. grated Parmesan cheese

Preparation

Place eggplant slices in a colander over a plate. Sprinkle with salt; toss. Let stand for 30 minutes. Rinse and drain well. Preheat oven to 450°. Spray a 9 x 13" baking pan with nonstick cooking spray. Layer eggplant, tomato and onion in prepared pan. Drizzle with 4 tablespoons melted butter; sprinkle with basil. Cover with aluminum foil and bake for 20 minutes. Arrange provolone cheese slices over vegetables. In a small bowl, stir together bread crumbs and remaining 2 tablespoons melted butter. Sprinkle crumb mixture over cheese slices. Sprinkle with Parmesan cheese. Bake uncovered for 10 minutes or until cheese is bubbly. Let stand for 10 minutes before serving.

Grilled Vegetable Parmesan

makes 6 to 8 servings

Ingredients

1 (1 lb.) eggplant,
sliced ¼" thick

2 fennel bulbs, trimmed,
sliced ¼" thick

1 sweet red bell pepper,
cut into thirds

1 sweet yellow bell pepper,
cut into thirds

1 sweet orange bell pepper,
cut into thirds

Olive oil for drizzling

Salt and pepper to taste

1 (24 oz.) jar marinara sauce

3 C. shredded mozzarella
cheese

1 C. grated Parmesan cheese

1 C. dry bread crumbs

Preparation

Preheat oven to 375°. Spray a 9 x 13" baking pan with nonstick cooking spray; set aside. Preheat grill to medium-high heat. In a large bowl, stir together eggplant, fennel and red, yellow and orange bell peppers; drizzle with olive oil and season with salt and pepper. Toss to coat vegetables. Grill vegetables for 3 to 4 minutes on each side or until softened. Pour ¾ cup marinara sauce in prepared pan. Arrange eggplant slices on top. Sprinkle with 1 cup mozzarella cheese and ⅓ cup Parmesan cheese. Arrange peppers in a single layer on top. Pour ¾ cup marinara sauce over peppers. Sprinkle with 1 cup mozzarella cheese and ⅓ cup Parmesan cheese. Arrange fennel on top and cover with remaining 1½ cups sauce. Sprinkle with remaining 1 cup mozzarella cheese and ⅓ cup Parmesan cheese. Sprinkle bread crumbs over cheese and drizzle with olive oil. Bake for 30 to 35 minutes or until golden brown. Let stand for 10 minutes before serving.

Desserts
&
Snacks

Berry Wonderful Bread Pudding

makes 12 servings

Ingredients

4 eggs
1 C. sugar
1½ tsp. vanilla extract
1 tsp. ground cinnamon
¼ C. melted butter, cooled

4 C. half-and-half
9 to 10 C. French or Italian bread cubes
1 to 2 C. fresh blueberries or blackberries

Preparation

Preheat oven to 300°. Spray a 9 x 13″ baking pan with nonstick cooking spray. Place pan in a larger baking pan with at least 1½″ sides; set aside. In a large mixing bowl, beat eggs and sugar on high speed for 4 to 5 minutes or until thick and lemon colored. Beat in vanilla and cinnamon until combined. Beat in melted and cooled butter and half-and-half. Place bread cubes and blueberries in prepared 9 x 13″ pan. Carefully pour egg mixture over bread cubes, completely covering bread with mixture. Set pans on center oven rack. Pour hot water into the larger pan until water is halfway up sides of 9 x 13″ pan. Bake for 1 hour or until a knife inserted near the center comes out clean. Remove 9 x 13″ pan from larger pan and cool slightly before serving.

Fruit 'n Nut Bread Pudding

makes 12 servings

Ingredients

16 slices day-old bread,
   torn into bite-size pieces
2 C. sugar
4 eggs
3 C. milk
2 tsp. ground cinnamon
½ tsp. salt

2 T. vanilla extract
1 (21 oz.) can apple pie filling
2 C. coarsely chopped pecans
1 C. golden raisins
¾ C. melted butter
Whipped cream, optional

Preparation

Preheat oven to 350°. Spray a 9 x 13″ baking pan with nonstick cooking spray; set aside. In a large bowl, stir together bread and sugar; set aside. In a medium mixing bowl, beat eggs, milk, cinnamon, salt and vanilla until foamy. Pour egg mixture over bread mixture and stir to mix well. Refrigerate for 2 hours. Stir in pie filling, pecans, raisins and butter. Pour mixture into prepared pan and bake for 45 to 50 minutes or until a knife inserted near the center comes out clean. Cool slightly and cut into squares. Serve warm or cold with whipped cream, if desired.

Creamy Cherry Cobbler

makes 8 to 12 servings

Ingredients

½ C. sliced almonds
1 C. plus 2 T. sugar, divided
2½ C. baking mix
1 C. sour cream

½ C. milk
¼ tsp. almond extract
2 (21 oz.) cans cherry pie filling
Vanilla ice cream, optional

Preparation

Preheat oven to 375°. Spray a 9 x 13″ baking pan with nonstick cooking spray; set aside. In a small bowl, stir together almonds and 2 tablespoons sugar; set aside. In a large bowl, mix together baking mix, remaining 1 cup sugar, sour cream, milk and almond extract until smooth. Spread batter in prepared pan. Spread pie filling evenly over batter. Bake for 35 to 40 minutes or until golden brown. Remove from oven and sprinkle with almond mixture. Return to oven and bake for 10 to 20 minutes more or until a toothpick inserted near the center comes out clean. Serve warm or cold with ice cream, if desired.

Apple & Cranberry Crisp

makes 8 to 12 servings

Ingredients

Butter for greasing
2½ to 3 lbs. Gala or
   Braeburn apples, peeled,
   cored, cut into ½" pieces
12 oz. fresh or frozen
   cranberries
1 C. sugar, divided
1¼ C. plus 3 T. flour, divided

1½ tsp. vanilla extract
¼ tsp. grated orange peel
1 T. orange juice
¾ tsp. ground cinnamon
¼ tsp. salt
⅛ tsp. ground allspice
⅛ tsp. ground nutmeg
10 T. butter, cubed

Preparation

Preheat oven to 375°. Grease a 9 x 13" baking pan with butter; set aside. In a large bowl, stir together apples, cranberries, ½ cup sugar, 3 tablespoons flour, vanilla, orange peel and orange juice. Transfer to prepared pan. In same bowl, stir together remaining 1¼ cups flour, remaining ½ cup sugar, cinnamon, salt, allspice and nutmeg. Use a pastry blender to cut in butter until mixture resembles coarse crumbs. Spread butter mixture over fruit mixture in pan. Bake for 55 to 60 minutes or until bubbly and topping is browned. Let cool for 15 minutes before serving.

Nectarine-Plum Cobbler

makes 8 to 12 servings

Ingredients

1¼ C. sugar, divided
2 T. cornstarch
¾ C. unsweetened apple juice
5 C. peeled, sliced fresh plums
5 C. peeled, sliced fresh
  nectarines

2½ C. flour
1 T. baking powder
½ tsp. baking soda
½ tsp. salt
½ C. butter, cubed
1½ C. buttermilk

Preparation

Preheat oven to 375°. Spray a 9 x 13˝ baking pan with nonstick cooking spray; set aside. In a large saucepan, combine ¾ cup sugar and cornstarch. Gradually whisk in apple juice until smooth. Stir in plums and nectarines. Cook and stir until mixture comes to a boil; cook 1 to 2 minutes more or until thickened and bubbly. Reduce heat to low; simmer for 5 minutes. Remove from heat; cool for 10 minutes and pour into prepared pan. In a large bowl, combine flour, baking powder, baking soda, salt and remaining ½ cup sugar. Use a pastry blender to cut in butter until mixture resembles coarse crumbs. Stir in buttermilk just until a soft dough forms. Drop by tablespoonfuls over fruit mixture. Bake for 30 to 35 minutes or until golden brown. Serve warm.

Chocolate Mint Freeze

makes 15 servings

Ingredients

1 (14 oz.) pkg. cream-filled chocolate sandwich cookies, crushed

¼ C. melted butter

1 (5 oz.) can evaporated milk

½ C. sugar

¼ C. butter, cubed

1 (1 oz.) square unsweetened baking chocolate

½ gal. mint chocolate chip ice cream, softened

1 (8 oz.) container whipped topping, thawed

Shaved chocolate, optional

Preparation

In a large bowl, combine cookie crumbs and melted butter. Press evenly in a 9 x 13″ pan. Refrigerate for 30 minutes. In a small saucepan over medium heat, combine milk, sugar, cubed butter and baking chocolate. Cook, stirring constantly, for 10 to 12 minutes or until thickened and bubbling. Remove from heat and cool completely. Spread ice cream evenly over cookie mixture in prepared pan. Spoon cooled chocolate mixture evenly over ice cream. Freeze until firm. Remove from freezer. Spread with whipped topping and garnish with shaved chocolate, if desired. Let stand for 10 minutes before cutting and serving.

Simply Delicious Ice Cream Dessert

makes 15 servings

Ingredients

17 miniature ice cream sandwiches, divided

1 (12.2 oz.) jar caramel ice cream topping

1 (12 oz.) container whipped topping, thawed

¼ C. chocolate syrup

1 (7 oz.) milk chocolate candy bar, chopped

Preparation

In a 9 x 13″ pan, arrange ice cream sandwiches in a single layer, cutting to fit as needed. Drizzle topping over ice cream sandwiches and spread with whipped topping. Drizzle with chocolate syrup and sprinkle with chopped candy bar. Cover and freeze for at least 1 hour. Cut into squares to serve.

Blackberry Sherbert

makes 1 quart

Ingredients

4 C. fresh or frozen, thawed
blackberries

2 C. sugar
2 C. buttermilk

Preparation

In a food processor bowl, combine blackberries and sugar; cover and process until smooth. Strain, discarding seeds and pulp. Stir in buttermilk. Transfer to a 9 x 13" pan and freeze for 1 hour or until edges begin to firm. Stir and return to freezer for at least 2 hours or until firm. Just before serving, transfer to a food processor bowl; cover and process for 2 to 3 minutes or until smooth.

Lemon Bars

makes 18 servings

Ingredients

2 C. plus 3 T. flour
½ C. powdered sugar, plus
   more for dusting
2 T. cornstarch
¼ tsp. salt
¾ C. butter

4 eggs, lightly beaten
1½ C. sugar
1 tsp. finely grated lemon peel
¾ C. lemon juice
¼ C. half-and-half

Preparation

Preheat oven to 350°. Line a 9 x 13″ baking pan with aluminum foil, allowing foil to extend 2″ beyond each end of pan. Spray the foil with nonstick cooking spray; set aside. In a large bowl, combine 2 cups flour, ½ cup powdered sugar, cornstarch and salt. Use a pastry blender to cut in butter until mixture resembles coarse crumbs. Press mixture in prepared pan. Bake for 18 to 20 minutes or until edges are golden brown. In a medium bowl, stir together eggs, sugar, remaining 3 tablespoons flour, lemon peel, lemon juice and half-and-half. Pour filling over hot crust. Bake for 15 to 20 minutes or until center is set. Cool in pan on a wire rack. Remove bars from pan using foil. Cut in squares, remove from foil and sift powdered sugar over the tops of bars before serving. Cover and store in the refrigerator.

Praline Bars

makes 24 servings

Ingredients

¾ C. butter, softened
1 C. sugar, divided
1 tsp. vanilla extract, divided
1½ C. flour

2 (8 oz.) pkgs. cream cheese, softened
2 eggs
½ C. toffee bits
3 T. caramel ice cream topping

Preparation

Preheat oven to 350°. In a large mixing bowl, combine butter, ½ cup sugar and ½ teaspoon vanilla on medium speed until light and fluffy. Gradually stir in flour, mixing on low speed until blended. Press in a 9 x 13″ baking pan and bake for 20 to 23 minutes or until lightly browned. In a medium mixing bowl, beat cream cheese, remaining ½ cup sugar and ½ teaspoon vanilla on medium speed until well blended. Add eggs and mix well. Stir in toffee bits and pour mixture over crust. Drizzle ice cream topping over all and lightly cut through batter with a knife to marble. Bake for 30 minutes more. Cool in pan on a wire rack. Cut into squares to serve.

Dark Chocolate Brownies

makes 12 servings

Ingredients

24 oz. dark baking chocolate
1 C. butter
4 eggs
2 C. sugar
2 T. vanilla extract

2 C. flour
1 tsp. baking powder
⅛ tsp. salt
¼ C. unsweetened cocoa
   powder

Preparation

Preheat oven to 350°. Spray a 9 x 13″ baking pan with nonstick cooking spray; set aside. In the top of a double boiler, combine baking chocolate and butter, stirring occasionally until melted. Add eggs, sugar and vanilla; mix thoroughly. In a small bowl, stir together flour, baking powder, salt and cocoa powder. Add to chocolate mixture; mix thoroughly. Transfer to prepared pan and bake for 45 minutes or until a toothpick inserted near the center comes out clean. Let cool on wire rack before serving.

Rocky Road Brownies

makes 12 servings

Ingredients

8 oz. unsweetened
   baking chocolate
1 C. butter
5 eggs
3½ C. sugar
2 tsp. instant espresso powder
1 T. vanilla extract

1⅔ C. flour
¼ tsp. salt
1½ C. semi-sweet chocolate
   chips, divided
2 C. chopped walnuts,
   toasted*, divided
2 C. miniature marshmallows

Preparation

Preheat oven to 400°. Spray a 9 x 13″ baking pan with nonstick cooking spray; set aside. In the top of a double boiler, combine baking chocolate and butter. Heat and stir until mixture is melted. Remove from heat; set aside. In a large mixing bowl, beat eggs, sugar and espresso powder on high speed for 5 minutes or until light and fluffy. Reduce speed to low. Add melted chocolate mixture and vanilla; beat until well combined. Slowly add flour and salt, beating until just blended. Fold in ½ cup chocolate chips and 1 cup toasted walnuts. Pour into prepared pan. Bake for 35 minutes or until edges are dry but center is soft. In a medium bowl, combine remaining 1 cup chocolate chips, 1 cup chopped walnuts and marshmallows. Sprinkle evenly over brownies. Return to oven and bake for 5 minutes more or until marshmallows are soft and lightly browned. Set on wire rack to cool for 20 minutes. Cut into squares and serve warm or at room temperature.

To toast, place walnuts in a dry skillet over medium heat and cook until browned, about 3 to 5 minutes, shaking pan often.

Zucchini Brownies

makes 12 servings

Ingredients

1 C. butter, softened
1½ C. sugar
2 eggs
½ C. plain yogurt
1 tsp. vanilla extract
2½ C. flour
¼ C. unsweetened
    cocoa powder

1 tsp. baking soda
½ tsp. salt
2 C. shredded zucchini
⅔ C. semi-sweet
    chocolate chips
½ C. creamy peanut butter

Preparation

Preheat oven to 350°. Spray a 9 x 13″ pan with nonstick cooking spray; set aside. In a large mixing bowl, cream together butter and sugar. Add eggs one at a time, beating well after each. Blend in yogurt and vanilla. In a medium bowl, stir together flour, cocoa powder, baking soda and salt; gradually add to creamed mixture. Fold in zucchini. Pour mixture into prepared pan. Bake for 35 to 40 minutes or until a toothpick inserted near the center comes out clean. In a small saucepan over low heat, combine chocolate chips and peanut butter. Cook and stir until smooth. Spread over warm brownies and cool in pan on a wire rack. Cut into squares before serving.

Honeyed Apple Spice Cake

makes 12 servings

Ingredients

¾ C. brown sugar
½ C. honey
⅓ C. butter, softened
4 eggs
½ C. cottage cheese
3 C. flour
2 tsp. ground cinnamon

1½ tsp. baking powder
1 tsp. salt
½ tsp. baking soda
¼ tsp. ground allspice
½ C. strong brewed
   coffee, cooled
1 C. peeled, diced apple

Preparation

Preheat oven to 350°. Spray a 9 x 13″ baking pan with nonstick cooking spray; set aside. In a large mixing bowl, beat brown sugar, honey and butter on medium speed until light and fluffy. Add eggs and cottage cheese; beat until creamy, scraping bowl if needed. Add flour, cinnamon, baking powder, salt, baking soda and allspice; beat on low speed until mixed. Continue to beat on low speed while adding coffee. Increase speed to medium and beat until creamy. Fold in apple. Transfer to prepared pan. Bake for 30 to 35 minutes or until a toothpick inserted near the center comes out clean. Cool for 30 minutes before cutting and serving.

Strawberry Delight

makes 15 servings

Ingredients

1½ C. graham cracker crumbs
½ C. sugar, divided
½ C. melted butter
1 (8 oz.) pkg. cream cheese, softened
3½ C. plus 2 T. milk, divided

1 (8 oz.) container whipped topping, thawed, divided
2 pints fresh strawberries, halved
2 (3.4 oz.) pkgs. vanilla instant pudding mix

Preparation

In a small bowl, mix together cracker crumbs, ¼ cup sugar and butter. Press firmly in a 9 x 13″ baking pan. Refrigerate while preparing filling. In a medium mixing bowl, beat cream cheese, remaining ¼ cup sugar and 2 tablespoons milk at medium speed until smooth. Gently stir in half of the whipped topping and spread over refrigerated mixture in pan. Top with strawberry halves. In a large bowl, combine remaining 3½ cups milk and pudding mixes. Beat with a wire whisk for 2 minutes or until well blended and thickened. Pour over strawberries. Refrigerate for several hours or until set. At serving time, spread with remaining half of the whipped topping.

Coconut Cream Dessert

makes 15 servings

Ingredients

1 C. flour
2 T. sugar
½ C. butter
½ C. chopped pecans
1 (8 oz.) pkg. cream cheese, softened
1 C. powdered sugar

1 (12 oz.) container whipped topping, thawed, divided
4 C. milk
3 (3.4 oz.) pkgs. coconut cream instant pudding mix
½ C. sweetened flaked coconut

Preparation

Preheat oven to 350°. Spray a 9 x 13″ baking pan with nonstick cooking spray; set aside. In a medium bowl, combine flour and sugar. Use a pastry blender to cut in butter until mixture resembles coarse crumbs. Stir in pecans. Press mixture in prepared pan. Bake for 20 to 25 minutes or until edges are lightly browned. Cool in pan on a wire rack. In a small mixing bowl, beat cream cheese and powdered sugar until smooth; fold in 1 cup whipped topping. Spread over crust. In a medium bowl, whisk together milk and pudding mixes for 2 minutes until well blended and thickened; let stand for 2 minutes. Spread pudding mixture over cream cheese mixture. Top with remaining 3¾ cups whipped topping; sprinkle with coconut. Refrigerate overnight. Cut into squares to serve.

3-Layer Pumpkin Dessert

makes 15 servings

Ingredients

1 (18.2 oz.) pkg. yellow
  cake mix
½ C. melted butter
3 eggs, divided
1 (30 oz.) can pumpkin
  pie filling

1 (5 oz.) can evaporated milk
½ C. sugar
¼ C. flour
1 T. ground cinnamon

Preparation

Preheat oven to 350°. Spray a 9 x 13˝ baking pan with nonstick cooking spray; set aside. In a large bowl, combine cake mix, butter and 1 egg until crumbly. Reserve ⅔ cup for topping. Press remaining mixture in prepared pan. In a large bowl, combine pie filling, milk and 2 beaten eggs; pour over crust. In a small bowl, stir together sugar, flour, cinnamon and reserved crumb mixture; sprinkle over pumpkin layer. Bake for 45 to 50 minutes or until top is golden brown. Cool in pan on a wire rack for 1 hour. Refrigerate for 2 hours before cutting and serving.

Candy Bar Dessert

makes 15 servings

Ingredients

2 C. chocolate wafer
  cookie crumbs
½ C. sugar, divided
½ C. melted butter
1 (8 oz.) pkg. cream
  cheese, softened

1 (12 oz.) container whipped
  topping, thawed, divided
1 C. chopped Snickers
  candy bars
3 C. milk
2 (3.9 oz.) pkgs. chocolate
  instant pudding

Preparation

In a 9 x 13″ pan, mix cookie crumbs, ¼ cup sugar and butter; press firmly onto bottom of pan and refrigerate. In a medium bowl, beat cream cheese and remaining ¼ cup sugar with a wire whisk until smooth. Gently stir in half of the whipped topping. Spread mixture evenly over crust. Sprinkle with chopped candy bars. In a large bowl, beat milk and pudding mixes with a wire whisk for 1 minute. Pour over mixture in pan. Let stand for 5 minutes or until pudding is thickened. Spread with remaining half of the whipped topping. Refrigerate until set before serving.

Creamy Cheesecake Bars

makes 20 to 24 servings

Ingredients

½ C. melted butter
1¼ C. sugar, divided
1¼ C. graham cracker crumbs*
3 (8 oz.) pkgs. cream cheese, softened
2 eggs

2 tsp. vanilla extract, divided
1½ tsp. lemon juice, divided
2 C. sour cream
1 (10 oz.) pkg. frozen fruit,** thawed, juice reserved
1 T. cornstarch

Preparation

Preheat oven to 350°. In a 9 x 13″ baking pan, stir together butter, ¼ cup sugar and cracker crumbs; press firmly onto bottom of pan. Bake for 8 minutes. Meanwhile, in a medium mixing bowl, beat cream cheese, eggs, ¾ cup sugar, 1 teaspoon vanilla and ½ teaspoon lemon juice on high speed until smooth and creamy. Remove pan from oven and pour cream cheese mixture over the crust. Return to oven and bake for 30 minutes more; cool completely. Preheat oven to 400°. In a small bowl, mix together sour cream, 2 tablespoons sugar and remaining 1 teaspoon vanilla. Pour over cooled cheesecake and bake for 5 minutes. Cool for several hours. Add enough water to reserved berry juice to make ¾ cup. In a 2-cup microwave-safe measuring cup, stir together remaining 2 tablespoons sugar and cornstarch. Stir in reserved juice and remaining 1 teaspoon lemon juice. Microwave on high for 3 to 5 minutes or until thick, stirring occasionally. Stir thickened juice mixture into fruit; cool completely. Pour over cheesecake and serve immediately.

Try using cinnamon-flavored graham crackers.

** *Strawberries, raspberries or blueberries work well*

Cheesecake Swirls

makes 20 to 24 servings

Ingredients

20 cream-filled chocolate
sandwich cookies, crushed
(about 2 C.)

3 T. melted butter

4 (8 oz.) pkgs. cream
cheese, softened

1 C. sugar

1 tsp. vanilla extract

1 C. sour cream

4 eggs

6 (1 oz.) squares semi-sweet
baking chocolate,
melted, cooled

Preparation

Preheat oven to 325°. Line a 9 x 13″ pan with aluminum foil, allowing foil to extend 2″ beyond each end of pan. In a large bowl, mix crushed cookies and butter; press firmly in prepared pan and bake for 10 minutes. In the same bowl, beat cream cheese, sugar and vanilla on medium speed until well blended. Add sour cream and mix well. Add eggs one at a time, beating on low speed after each addition until just combined. Remove 1 cup batter and set aside. Stir melted chocolate into remaining batter in bowl; pour over crust. Top with spoonfuls of set-aside plain batter and cut through both layers several times with a knife to swirl. Bake for 40 minutes or until center is almost set. Cool. Refrigerate overnight. Remove bars from pan using foil and cut in squares. Remove from foil before serving. Store in refrigerator.

Eggnog Cheesecake Squares

makes 20 to 24 servings

Ingredients

1¾ C. buttery cracker crumbs
¾ C. sugar, divided
1⅛ tsp. ground nutmeg, divided
⅓ C. melted butter

3 (8 oz.) pkgs. cream cheese, softened
1 tsp. vanilla extract
2 eggs
1 C. eggnog

Preparation

Preheat oven to 350°. In a 9 x 13″ baking pan, mix cracker crumbs, ¼ cup sugar, ½ teaspoon nutmeg and butter. Press firmly in pan and bake for 8 minutes; remove from oven. In a large mixing bowl, beat cream cheese on medium speed until smooth. Add ½ cup sugar, vanilla and ½ teaspoon nutmeg. Beat until combined. Add eggs one at a time, beating on medium speed after each addition until just combined. Stir in eggnog. Pour mixture over crust and bake for 22 minutes or until almost set. Cool in pan on a wire rack for 1 hour. Sprinkle with remaining ⅛ teaspoon nutmeg. Refrigerate for at least 2 hours. Cut into squares to serve.

Candy Cane Squares

makes 20 to 24 servings

Ingredients

1¾ C. graham cracker crumbs

3 T. sugar

⅓ C. melted butter

1¼ C. semi-sweet chocolate chips

1¾ C. whipping cream, divided

2 (8 oz.) pkgs. cream cheese, softened

1¼ C. powdered sugar

1½ tsp. peppermint extract

½ tsp. vanilla extract

Red food coloring, optional

1 C. coarsely crushed peppermint candy canes

24 small peppermint candy canes, optional

Preparation

In a 9 x 13″ pan, stir together cracker crumbs, sugar and butter; press firmly onto bottom of pan and refrigerate. In a small saucepan over low heat, stir together chocolate chips and ¾ cup whipping cream. Cook and stir until smooth; pour over crust and refrigerate. In a large mixing bowl, beat cream cheese, powdered sugar, peppermint extract and vanilla on medium speed until fluffy. Beat in food coloring to desired shade. Gradually add remaining 1 cup whipping cream, beating on high speed until fluffy. Fold in crushed candy canes and spread mixture over chocolate layer. Refrigerate for 2 hours. At serving time, cut into squares and top each with a small candy cane, if desired. Store in refrigerator.

Famous Strawberry Pretzel Dessert

makes 20 to 24 servings

Ingredients

2 C. finely crushed pretzels
½ C. sugar, divided
⅔ C. melted butter
1½ (8 oz.) pkgs. cream
  cheese, softened

2 T. milk
1 C. whipped topping, thawed
1 (6 oz.) pkg. strawberry
  gelatin
4 C. fresh sliced strawberries

Preparation

Preheat oven to 350°. In a 9 x 13″ baking pan, stir together crushed pretzels, ¼ cup sugar and butter; press firmly onto bottom of pan. Bake for 10 minutes and cool. In a medium mixing bowl, beat cream cheese, remaining ¼ cup sugar and milk on medium speed until well blended. Stir in whipped topping and spread mixture over crust; refrigerate. In a large bowl, add 2 cups boiling water to gelatin; stir for 2 minutes or until completely dissolved. Stir in 1½ cups cold water. Refrigerate gelatin for 1½ hours or until thickened. Add strawberries to thickened gelatin; spoon gelatin mixture over cream cheese mixture. Refrigerate until firm. Cut into squares to serve.

Index

Breakfasts

Salads

Side Dishes

Main Dishes

Meatless Main Dishes

Desserts & Snacks